FAMILIES ENCOURAGING FAITH

A Parents' Guide to
the Young Adult Years

Jerrie Ann Goewey
and Kenneth Goewey

THE WORLD OF
DON BOSCO
MULTIMEDIA

NEW ROCHELLE, NY

Families Encouraging Faith: A Parents' Guide to the Young Adult Years is published as part of the Catholic Families Series—resources to promote faith growth in Families.
Materials available for parish and diocesan leaders, parents and families

Available titles:

For leaders and ministers:
Families and Young Adults
Families and Youth
Families and Young Adolescents
Growing in Faith: A Catholic Family Sourcebook
Media, Faith, and Families: A Parish Ministry Guide
Rituals for Sharing Faith: A Resource for Parish Ministers
Faith and Families: A Parish Program for Parenting in Faith Growth

For parents and families:
Families Nurturing Faith: A Parents' Guide to the Preschool Years
Families Sharing Faith: A Parents' Guide to the Grade School Years
Families Experiencing Faith: A Parents' Guide to the Young Adolescent Years
Families Exploring Faith: A Parents' Guide to the Older Adolescent Years
Media, Faith, and Families: A Parents' Guide to Family Viewing
Family Rituals and Celebrations

The Catholic Families Series is a publishing project of Don Bosco Multimedia and the Center for Youth Ministry Development

Families Encouraging Faith: A Parents' Guide to the Young Adult Years
©1992 Salesian Society, Inc. / Don Bosco Multimedia
475 North Ave., P.O. Box T, New Rochelle, NY 10802

Library of Congress Cataloging-in-Publication Data
Families Encouraging Faith: A Parents' Guide to the Young Adult Years /
     Jerrie Ann Goewey and Kenneth Goewey
p. cm. — Catholic Families Series
Includes bibliographical references.
     1. Family life 2. Religious development
          I. Goewey, Jerrie Ann. II. Goewey, Kenneth.
ISBN 0-89944-253-6 $6.95

Design and Typography by Sally Ann Zegarelli, Long Branch, NJ 07740

Printed in the United States of America

6/92   9 8 7 6 5 4 3 2 1

PREFACE

FAMILIES ENCOURAGING FAITH: A PARENTS' GUIDE TO THE YOUNG ADULT YEARS

A quick look at the family section of your local bookstore will reveal dozens of books about parenting. What you probably will not find among these titles is a book about parenting and faith growth. To fill this void, we have created five books which help parents of children from the pre-school years through the young adult years nurture the faith growth of their children. These new titles are part of the Catholic Families Series published by Don Bosco Multimedia.

Even though you may consider your parenting job completed as your child moves through young adulthood, the good news is that you can continue to have an influence on your young adult's faith and values and grow with them in the process.

Families Encouraging Faith is specifically designed for parents of young adults. It provides you with an understanding of the unique characteristics of young adults and their families at this stage of life. It outlines the possibilities for sharing faith with young adults through the authors' personal stories and through specific strategies and activities. It also suggests ways that you can continue your growth in faith.

Our hope is to promote opportunities for families with young adults to continue the faith sharing and faith growth which began in childhood. We hope you find the stories, insights, and ideas a source of support and encouragement as you continue parenting.

ABOUT THE AUTHORS

Jerrie Ann and Kenneth Goewey have been married for over 30 years and have four children. Ken has been the owner of his own business. He and Jerrie Ann are co-directors of the Family Life Office of the Diocese of Albany, NY. They are members of the National Association of Catholic Family Life Ministers and were New York State representatives to the Board of Directors. They assisted in the production of the book *Newlymarried Ministry—A Statement of Principles and Guidelines*. Jerrie Ann hosts a monthly TV show, which she and Ken co-produce, called *Partners—Family, Church, Society*.

CONTENTS

1

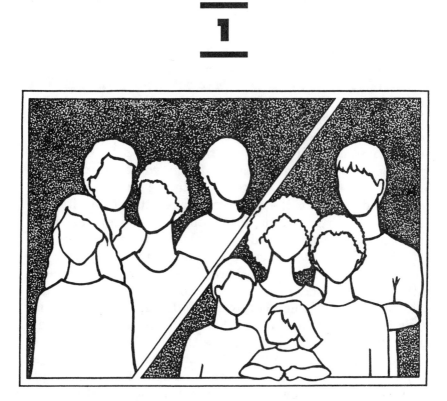

PARENTING FOR FAITH GROWTH TODAY

WHY FAMILIES NEED FAITH

As every good parent knows, parenting involves much more than providing basic food and shelter, education and health care. Parenting is also about loving and caring, building self-esteem and a sense of values. Effective parenting helps children understand how they relate to others and what they can do to make the world a better place for themselves and for all people.

Parenting is a shared task. Despite all the different shapes that families come in today—single-parent and two-parent, blended and extended—the challenge of parenting

1

continues to be shared across generations and across family lines. Grandparents, aunts and cousins share in the task, as do special friends who have become "family" for us in a different way. People of faith proclaim that God is also an active partner with them in their job of parenting.

Faith provides family members with shared beliefs and values to guide their life together and to direct their involvement beyond the family circle. Faith values nurture the family's well-being and provide it with the criteria needed to weigh and evaluate the many messages that come its way each day. Faith proclaims, for example, that every person is endowed by God with dignity and blessed with a unique mix of gifts and talents. These gifts and talents, in turn, are meant to be shared with others. This vision of personhood calls families to recognize, nurture and celebrate the uniqueness of each family member. It also calls families to recognize their interdependence with others and to share the talents and gifts nurtured in family life with others in their community and world. As simple as this faith value seems, it often stands in sharp contrast to societal messages that judge people in light of what they have or that promote isolation from others who seem, at least at first glance, to be different from us.

As parents model faith values at home and in the community, nurture a sense of dignity and uniqueness in their children and encourage family members to share their talents with others, they join with God in the sacred task of building a world based on gospel values. Children, in turn, take what they have learned and practiced at home and carry it into the world, guaranteeing a new generation committed to creating a world based on gospel values.

Faith serves, as well, as a source of comfort and strength for parents, assuring them that they are not alone in the task of parenting and providing them with a special Friend to whom they can turn for direction and support. As parents join with their God in the task of parenting, they come to realize that there are no social, geographical or educational barriers to good parenting. Good parenting does not depend upon a high hourly wage, a prestigious address or the number of degrees after a person's name. You don't have to be a biological parent to develop a strong family life. You can be an adoptive parent, a single parent, a parent of healthy or handicapped children. Good parenting is possible for all people who trust enough in themselves, in the other members of their families and in their God.

Faith provides people with the values and vision needed to live life fully. Families need faith to survive and thrive in today's world. Our challenge in this book is to offer you and your family practical insights and strategies for developing a meaningful faith life.

KEYS TO EFFECTIVE PARENTING

Before we begin this book on parenting for faith growth and turn to the descriptions and suggestions offered by our authors, it will be important to look at the adventure of parenting today and what we mean by parenting for faith growth.

As noted above, the key to effective parenting lies within you. Your drive to make your family the best that it can be need not be blocked by your particular life circumstances. To be sure, your path may be more winding and littered than some, but effectiveness in parenting is an internal quality, not easily squashed by external conditions. It is a desire to make the most of yourself and your family, whatever your talents or situation.

What do we know about effective parenting? Who can we turn to for advice? One of the best sources for our wisdom about parenting is to turn to other parents. In *Back to the Family*, Dr. Ray Guarendi gathered the shared wisdom of one hundred of America's happiest and most effective families. He shares the following thoughts on what makes families effective:[1]

1.   **A strong home life does not depend upon a parent's education, occupation, ethnicity or social status.** Neither is it limited to biological parents, two-parent homes or a low-stress

existence. Effective parenting and a strong home life are not the product of external causes but are born internally. They evolve from commitment, from determination to build upon your family's strengths, regardless of what factors may be pulling against you.

2.   Successful parents are not all products of successful childhoods. While many parents knew upbringings filled with positive examples from which to anchor their own parenting, others have lived through childhoods best described as cold, abusive or even traumatic. Parents who have risen far above their childhoods are living proof that, contrary to some experts' opinions, the quality of your past does not put a ceiling on the quality of your present as a parent or as a person.

3.   Effective parents are not perfect or even close to perfect. They wrestle with worries, insecurities and guilts all parents feel. They don't have all the answers, endless patience or perfect children. Their lives reveal that skillful parenting is not inborn. It is developed over time, along with a healthy acceptance of one's imperfections. Better parenting results from recognizing our limits and working to overcome them or live with them.

4. Good parents love to parent. They've experienced the challenges and fears inherent to childrearing and remain grateful for the opportunity to be parents. Lifestyles and priorities can change radically with the decision to raise children. Responsible parents accept this reality, even welcome it.

5.   Common sense and good judgment form the foundation for sound parenting decisions. Having discovered that no one right way exists for handling any situation, effective parents strive for self-confidence. It leads to more decisive parenting and more secure children. Childrearing is a never-ending process. It is drawing upon the knowledge and experience of others—children, parents and experts. The willingness to learn from others is indispensable to better parenting, but ultimately you must judge for yourself what will work for your family, based upon your values and unique circumstances.

6. **A parent's personality has far more influence on her childrearing than being aware of all the latest child-rearing trends.** Work to become a better person and your parenting will automatically improve.

7. **Wise parents are open to guidance from their children.** Children are natural teachers of childrearing. They know us well—in many ways, better than anyone else does. Since they are with us every day, they are ready and able to give us feedback on our technique. Living mirrors, they reflect back at us who we are, what we act like, what we sound like. Lessons most basic to successful parenting are taught by children:

- *Show your love.* At the heart of all quality parenting is unconditional love. No matter what our children do, our love for them will never cease. Unconditional love is the basis for every parenting decision and action. It is the driving force behind all discipline.

- *Teach through example; practice what you preach.*

- *Listen before you talk.*

- *Look through a child's eyes.* Children do not see parenthood through the eyes of parents.

8. **A relaxed parent is a better parent.** How fully we enjoy our children is directly related to two factors: a relaxed attitude toward childrearing and being prepared for the inevitable rough times that every parent faces. There are ways to parent more calmly right now. Enjoyable childrearing begins with accepting several parenting facts of life. These are truths at the very heart of parenthood.

- *Don't try to be a perfect parent.* Undeserved anxiety and guilt will follow.

- *Don't fear mistakes.* They are necessary for maturation. Good parents become better through mistakes.

■ *Parent in the present.* Second guessing yourself or dwelling on the uncertain future will erode your confidence and ability to give your best to your children today.

■ *Expect that your children will misunderstand and dislike you at times.* That is a reality of responsible parenthood.

■ *Laugh whenever and wherever you can during childrearing.* Humor helps maintain perspective and eases anxiety.

9. Spiritual beliefs are a dominant presence in strong families. Faith in a Creator and in living by God's guidelines provide values which nurture each member's personal growth and thereby the family's. Spirituality fosters parenting through example, the most durable parenting. It is a source of comfort and strength, enabling parents to call upon a supreme authority for wisdom and direction.

10. There are no shortcuts to strong family life. A parent must invest time. Dedication means a willingness to give quantity time, which is necessary for quality time. Time provides the framework for all elements of family success—communication, discipline, values. Making family a priority fosters a child's self-esteem and sense of belonging. Nothing is more precious to a child than the presence of a parent.

11. Competent parents concentrate on mastering the basics of communication. A few good principles guide them:

■ *Talk less at children and listen more to them.* Attentive silence is the simplest way to evoke a child's feelings.

■ *Become sensitive to children's prime times to talk.* Arrange them or be present when they occur. They are windows into their thoughts.

■ *Affection is continuous communication.* It is love without words. Strong families know the binding power of affection.

- *Whenever possible, allow children a voice in family decisions.* While in most cases, parents retain the final say, merely being consulted makes a child feel an integral part of the family.

12. Responsible parents expect much of their children and of themselves. Their attitude is, "Success is not measured against others but against yourself. Striving for your personal best is a success." Parents counsel:

- *Insist on your children's full effort in academics.* It is their future.

- *The family home is everyone's home, so make it everyone's responsibility,* down to the youngest members.

- *Judge children's capabilities—social, emotional, personal—and expect them to live up to them.* Don't allow them to live down to the norm.

13. Strong parents believe in strong discipline begun young. They are willing to exert whatever effort is necessary to discipline their children today so life won't discipline them tomorrow. The firmest parent, if loving, is a more gentle teacher than the world. For a child's sake, parents need the will to discipline. The best discipline is motivated by unconditional love, love that is unaffected by a child's misbehavior. Good disciplinarians focus most on what children do right, not wrong. They emphasize the positive. Not only does this make for less discipline, it enhances a child's self image. By their nature, children test limits and want more than is healthy for them. Loving parents are not afraid to say no. They draw clear boundaries within which a child is free to operate.

The mechanics of effective discipline are summarized by the three C's: calm, consistency and consequences. Calm discipline works more quickly and leads to less regrettable behavior from everyone. Consistency is predictability. It enables children to understand and accept the results of their actions. Consequences, not words, are the basic tools of discipline.

14. Strong families rely on simple, clear-cut home rules enforced by consequences. They derive some of their stability from house rules. Established according to a family's needs and goals, rules make for a more content household. The content of the rules changes as the family evolves, but their purpose remains the constant: to promote mutual respect, responsibility and a more pleasant environment for everyone.

Refined to its most basic elements, successful parenting is unconditional love, commitment, teaching by example and the will to discipline. Effective parenting is an attainable reality. Build upon the essentials, and no level of family success is beyond your reach. In this book we will be encouraging you to utilize these ingredients of effective parenting by suggesting practical insights and skills for parenting young adults.

THE FAMILY AS A LIVING SYSTEM

No human being grows in a vacuum. To be human is, by definition, to be interdependent, to rely on others for the support and assistance needed to grow to full life. No place is this more apparent than in the life of the family. Family members depend upon one another and have a tremendous impact on one another's growth. Change and growth in any family member's life automatically impacts all other family members. If a major change occurs in the life of a single family member, all members are forced to adjust to the change. This can entail adjustments in the relationships among individual family members or a recasting of what it means to be family together.

Researchers use the term "system" to describe the organic relationship that exists between individual family members and the family as a whole. You may remember from high school science classes that living organisms and their environments function as a system. All living systems attempt to maintain *equilibrium* or balance. When a change takes place that upsets this balance, the system responds by doing something to restore the equilibrium that existed previously.

The family is a system, too—a system in which relationships change in response to the changing needs and concerns of family members and in response to changes in the family's relationship with the larger society. And like other systems, families attempt to maintain a sense of equilibrium in their relationships. Certain understandings develop regarding roles, rules, relationships and responsibilities in the family. These understandings form the system by which the family operates. Often times, families are unaware of how these roles, rules, relationships and responsibilities affect their entire life as a family.

The tendency for family systems to try to maintain their established patterns of behavior is challenged from time to time by changes to which they must adapt. These changes can be a regular part of the family's growth and development. The birth of the first child causes an imbalance in the family system of the couple, often making many of the former roles, rules, relationships and responsibilities unworkable. The arrival of adolescence brings with it periods of imbalance as formerly accepted roles, rules, relationships and responsibilities are questioned by the adolescent. During these life transitions it is *healthy* for family roles, rules, relationships and responsibilities to change, for through such changes families adjust to the changes and restore a new balance to the system.

Sometimes these changes are brought about by major events in the life of the family, such as the loss of a parent through death or divorce or the remarriage of parents resulting in a new blended family. The members of a family must find ways to reorganize and reestablish workable roles, rules, relationships and responsibilities in light of these major life events. Such changes often result in longer periods of imbalance as the family system seeks to adjust to the changes and establish a new balance. Making changes during these major events is difficult, but it is *healthy*. Families need to adjust to the new situation they face and restore a new balance to the system. Only in this way can the family feel comfortable again.

At other times, you as the parent may wish to make a change in the family by introducing new ways of relating, new patterns of family living, new rules, new practices, etc. In this book we introduce you to a variety of ways to share faith with your children. You may want to use many of these new ideas in your family. Be aware that family members often resist change, not because the changes are bad, but because change is upsetting. It causes anxiety. When a family establishes its balance, members are comfortable with the status quo. Anything new, even if positive, will likely be resisted, and a subtle message of "change back" will be communicated. Change requires at least three steps: the change itself, the family's reaction to the change and dealing with the family's reaction to the change. By understanding how your family system works (what the roles, rules, relationship patterns and responsibilities are), you can be prepared for your family's reaction. For example, you can identify what needs to change in order to introduce the idea, involve family members in deciding and planning for the change, keep communication lines open during the change, suggest that they try the new idea for a specific length of time and then evaluate, etc.

HOW FAMILIES GROW

Today it has become commonplace to talk about the changes we experience throughout our lives. We are aware of the differing life tasks and characteristics of childhood, adolescence, young adulthood, middle adulthood and later adulthood. Each of these "stages" or times of life brings with it new challenges and important life tasks to accomplish. In a family both children and parents are experiencing their own individual journeys.

We may not be as fully aware that the family as a unit or system has important life tasks to address and needs and functions to fulfill. A family in its "infancy" is different from a family in its "adolescence." Like individuals, families move through a life cycle, a family life cycle—that is, various stages in which new issues arise and different concerns predominate. During the first years of marriage, for example, families focus nearly all their energy on establishing a household, finding suitable employment and strengthening the marital relationship. During the child-bearing stage, the family's concerns shift to taking care of their young children. Families are likely to have higher medical expenses, more debts in general and concerns about managing work and family commitments. During the "young adult" stage, when children begin leaving home, families are usually less strained financially, and their concerns shift to reorganizing the household in response to their children's departure. Each stage of the family life cycle is different from those that came before and those that will follow.

These family life cycle changes are a regular part of the family's growth and development. Consequently, in order to understand the changing nature of family relationships throughout the family life cycle, we must take into account not only characteristics of the developing child or adolescent or young adult, but characteristics of the parents and of the family as a system at each stage of life.

A family life cycle perspective sees the family as a three or four generational system moving through time in a life cycle of distinct stages. During each stage the family is confronted with particular tasks to accomplish and challenges to face in order to prepare itself and its members for further growth and development. Viewing family life through a systems perspective can be a powerful tool for helping people understand what is happening in the life of their family and for creating strategies that promote individual and family faith growth and sharing.

Starting with the new couple, the following brief paragraphs describe the tasks faced by families at each stage of development. While no single development theory can explain all the factors that contribute to individual and family growth, such theories do provide windows through which we can gain a better understanding of how families change and grow. They help us understand what is happening in the life of the individual and in the life of the family as a whole.[2]

NEW COUPLE

Marriage joins not just two individuals, but two families together in a new relationship. It presents the new couple with a series of new challenges, including:

- defining and learning the role of husband and wife;

- establishing new relationships as a couple with their families of origin and with their friends;

- developing a commitment to a new family, with its own rules, roles, responsibilities, values and traditions.

As they confront these challenges, the new couple often finds themselves reflecting on the influence of their family of origin to draw insights, values and traditions that they want to include in their new family. This reflection helps them to sort out emotionally what they will take along from the family of origin, what they will leave behind and what they will create for themselves.

FAMILIES WITH CHILDREN

With the birth of the first child, the couple embarks on a new life task—to accept new members into the family and to adjust the rules, roles, responsibilities and relationships of their family to include the needs of the youngest members. The challenge for families with children involves:

- developing parenting roles and skills;

- negotiating and joining in childrearing, financial and household tasks;

- realigning relationships with extended family to include grandparenting roles;

- sharing socialization with the outside world;

- developing new patterns of family communication, traditions, celebrations.

FAMILIES WITH ADOLESCENTS

Adolescence ushers in a new era in family life brought on by new adolescent life tasks and the changing role of the parents in relationship to their adolescent children. The changes of adolescence—puberty, new ways of thinking, wider sphere of social activity and relationships, greater autonomy— present the family as a whole with a new set of challenges. In fact, it would be fair to say that the whole family experiences adolescence. The challenge for families with adolescents involves:

- allowing for the increasing independence of adolescents, while maintaining enough structure to foster continued family development;

- reflection by adult members on their personal, marital and career life issues;

- adjusting patterns of family communication, traditions, celebrations;

- and for some families beginning the shift toward joint caring for the older generation.

The task for most families with adolescents—and it is by no means an easy one—is to maintain *emotional* involvement, in the form of concern and caring, while gradually moving toward a relationship characterized by greater *behavioral* autonomy.

FAMILIES WITH YOUNG ADULTS

The most significant aspect of this stage of life is that it is marked by the greatest number of exits and entries of family members. The stage begins with the launching of grown children into schooling, careers and homes of their own, and proceeds with the entry of their spouses and children. The challenge for families with young adults involves:

- regrouping as a family as each young adult moves out from the family;

- changes in the marital relationship now that parenting responsibilities are no longer required;

- development of adult-to-adult relationships between grown children and their parents;

- realigning relationships to include in-laws and grand-children;

- caring for the older generation and dealing with disabilities and death.

This stage of family life also presents unique challenges to the young adult, for example:

- accepting emotional and financial responsibility for oneself;

- formulating personal life goals;

- developing intimate peer relationships;

- establishing oneself in the world of work.

FAMILIES IN LATER LIFE

Among the tasks of families in later life is the adjustment to retirement, which not only may create the obvious vacuum for the retiring person, but may put a special strain on the marriage. Financial insecurity and dependence are also special difficulties, especially for family members who value managing for themselves. And while loss of friends and relatives is a particular difficulty at this phase, the loss of a spouse is the most difficult adjustment, with its problems of reorganizing one's entire life alone after many years as a couple and of having fewer relationships to help replace the loss. Grandparenthood can, however, offer a new lease on life and opportunities for special close relationships without the responsibilities of parenthood.

In this book we will describe many of the major characteristics and concerns of the growing young adult, as well as
those of parents and the family as a whole. These explana-
tions will help you to understand the changing nature of
family relationships during young adulthood and to offer
practical suggestions for parenting and faith growth in
families with young adults.

HOW FAMILIES GROW IN FAITH

The Christian vision of family life speaks about the family as
a community of life and love. It proclaims that family life is
sacred and that family activities are holy, that God's love is
revealed and communicated in new ways each and every day
through Christian families. This Christian vision of family life
calls families to a unique identity and mission. This means
that the Christian family has several important responsibilities as it seeks to grow in faith:

- *Families form a loving community.*
  Families work to build a community based on love,
  compassion, respect, forgiveness and service to others. In
  families, people learn how to give and receive love and
  how to contribute to the good of other family members. In
  families, people open themselves to experiencing God's
  love through their dealings with one another, through the
  ethnic and cultural values and traditions that are part of
  family life and through the events of family life.

- *Families serve life by bearing and educating children.*
  Families serve life by bringing children into the world, by
  handing on Catholic Christian values and traditions and
  by developing the potential of each member at every age.
  As parents and all family members share their values
  with one another, they grow toward moral and spiritual
  maturity.

- *Families participate in building a caring and just society.*
  Families participate in building a caring and just society.

The gospel values of service, compassion and justice are first learned and practiced in families. In Christian families people learn how to reach out beyond the home to serve those in need and to work for justice for all God's people. How family members learn to relate to each other with respect, love, caring, fidelity, honesty and commitment becomes their way of relating to others in the world.

- *Families share in the life and mission of the Church.* Families share in the life and mission of the Church when the gospel vision and values are communicated and applied in daily life, when faith is celebrated through family rituals or through participation in the sacramental life of the church, when people gather as a family or parish community to pray, when people reach out, in Jesus' name, in loving service to others.

These responsibilities may sound overwhelming and unrealistic given all your other responsibilities as parents. In this book we will use these four responsibilities to develop practical ideas that you can use to share faith and promote individual and family faith growth. We will organize our ideas around six time-honored ways of sharing faith: (1) sharing the Catholic faith story, (2) celebrating faith through rituals, (3) praying together, (4) enriching family relationships, (5) responding to those in need through actions of justice and service, and (6) relating to the wider community.

Sharing the Catholic faith story happens when parents share stories from the Scriptures with their children, when families discuss the implications and applications of Christian faith for daily living, when a moral dilemma is encountered and the family turns to the resources of the Catholic faith for guidance, when parents discuss the religious questions their young adults ask. The family's sharing is complemented by participation of children, parents and/or the entire family in the catechetical program of the parish community.

Celebrating faith through rituals happens when the family celebrates the liturgical year, such as Advent and

Christmas, Lent and Easter; celebrates the civic calendar, like Martin Luther King, Jr. Day and Earth Day; celebrates milestones or rites of passages, such as birthdays, anniversaries, graduations, special recognitions; celebrates ethnic traditions which have been passed down through the generations; celebrates the rituals of daily life, like meal prayer and forgiveness. These celebrations provide the foundations for a family ritual life in which God is discovered and celebrated through the day, week, month and year. The family's ritual life is complemented by participation in the ritual life of the parish community with its weekly celebration of the Eucharist; regular sacramental celebrations, such as Reconciliation and Anointing of the Sick; and liturgical year celebrations.

Praying together as a family is a reality when families incorporate prayer into the daily living through meal and bed times, times of thanksgiving and of crisis; when parents teach basic prayers and pray with their children. The family's prayer life is complemented by participation in the communal prayer life of the parish community, especially through liturgical year celebrations.

Enriching family relationships occurs when the family spends both quality and quantity time together; participates in family activities; works at developing healthy communication patterns which cultivate appreciation, respect and support for each other; negotiates and resolves problems and differences in positive and constructive ways. Enriching family relationships also involves the parents in developing their marriage relationship or a single parent developing intimate, supportive relationships in his or her life.

Performing acts of justice and service takes place when the family recognizes the needs of others in our communities and in our world and seeks to respond. Families act through stewardship and care for the earth; through direct service to others, the homeless and the hungry; through study of social issues; through developing a family lifestyle based on equality, nonviolence, respect for human dignity, respect for the earth. The family's service involvement is strengthened when it is done together with other families in the parish community.

Relating as a family to the wider community happens when families join together in family support groups or family clusters for sharing, activities and encouragement; when families learn about the broader church and world, especially the cultural heritages of others in the community or the world; when families organize to address common concerns facing them in the community, like quality education or safe neighborhoods.

This is quite a challenge for the family! Don't be over-whelmed. What is essential is that you identify how you already share faith using these six ways and try new approaches that will enrich your family life. In this book we have included ideas to support your current efforts and to encourage you to try new ways to share faith. Adapt and revise these ideas so that they work for you.

Remember that the family shares responsibility with the parish community for promoting faith growth in each of these six ways. A careful look at the six ways will reveal the basic functions of the parish community, e.g., religious education, sacraments and worship, serving the needs of others. The parish and family approach each of these six ways of sharing faith differently. The parish community needs to support and encourage the efforts of families to share faith. Families need to be involved in the life of the parish community so that their family efforts can be connected to the larger community of faith. Don't be afraid to challenge your parish community and its leaders to support families and to offer programs and services for families that will promote the family's growth in faith.

GROWING TOWARD MATURITY IN FAITH

What do we hope will happen in the lives of family members—parents and children alike—if we strengthen our efforts at sharing faith? It is our hope that family members will discover meaning and purpose for their lives in a life-trans-forming relationship with a loving God in Jesus Christ and a consistent devotion to serving others as Jesus did.

Our growth as Catholic Christians is never complete. It is a life-long journey towards greater maturity in faith. While no complete description of this journey is possible, we hope and pray that you and your family will grow toward a living faith characterized by the following elements:

- trusting in God's saving grace and firmly believing in the humanity and divinity of Jesus Christ;

- experiencing a sense of personal well-being, security and peace;

- integrating faith and life—seeing work, family, social relationships and political choices as part of your religious life;

- seeking spiritual growth through Scripture, study, reflection, prayer and discussion with others;

- seeking to be part of a Catholic community of believers in which people give witness to their faith, support and nourish one another, serve the needs of each other and the community, and worship together;

- developing a deeper understanding of the Catholic Christian tradition and its applicability to life in today's complex society;

- holding life-affirming gospel values, including respect for human dignity, commitment to uphold human rights, equality (especially racial and gender), steward-ship, care and compassion and a personal sense of responsibility for the welfare of others;

- advocating for social and global change to bring about greater social justice and peace;

- serving humanity, consistently and passionately, through acts of love and justice.

Families provide a natural context for nurturing God's gift of faith. As families and individuals grow together in faith, life is enriched and the gospel vision brought closer to reality. Faith and family are a natural duo. May this volume be one small step toward helping you grow together more effectively.

End Notes

[1] These points about effective parenting were summarized from *Back to the Family* by Ray Guarendi (New York: Villard Books, 1990).

[2] The family life cycle perspective described below was adapted from "The Family Life Cycle," by Betty Carter and Monica McGoldrick in *Growing in Faith: A Catholic Family Sourcebook,* ed. John Roberto (New Rochelle: Don Bosco Multimedia, 1990.)

2

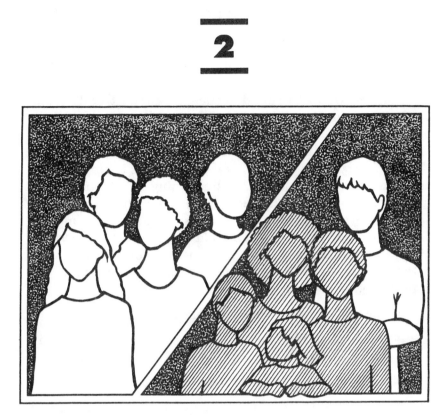

UNDERSTANDING FAMILIES WITH YOUNG ADULTS

Families are much like the seasons—spring, summer, winter, fall. Each has a natural, expected ebb and flow—cycles or stages that we grow and work through as individuals and together, as a family. And just as each season has its strengths and drawbacks, families also have joys and sorrows, crises and peace.

We live these seasons as we pray, laugh and work our way through our children leaving home, our own mid-life issues and the issues of our aging parents. The particular season of life we are speaking about in these pages is families with young adults. What we are experiencing at this point in time are various exits and entries into and from our family system. This season or stage continues from the time the first child leaves home until the last child leaves home.

Anyone who has raised teenagers knows the difficulty parents have in remaining stable during these years and the importance of doing so for their children. Now that our children are entering adulthood, we, as mid-life parents, face the task of trying to cope with all the changes taking place in our lives, in our children's lives as young adults and in the lives of our parents. The tasks involved in help our young adult children establish their own lives and in moving forward on our journey of emotional and spiritual development are challenging—even though they look simple when listed. The tasks include responsibilities to our children, our parents and ourselves:

- renegotiating our marital relationship;
- developing adult-to-adult relationships with our children;
- making room for in-laws and grandchildren;
- dealing with the limitations of aging in our parents and their eventual death.

Pretty clear and understandable, right? Living them out is when we, as parents, find the simple becomes complex and the understandable becomes confusing. Perhaps this is because we have the ideal image of what family should be. The expectation is of smooth sailing, of all for one and one for all, loving attitudes, thoughts and behavior at all times. Our family should be like a Norman Rockwell painting—soft and warm with everyone feeling close and loved.

Now let's take a look at what the reality is for most families. Families come in many different sizes and shapes, with different histories and different expectations of what it means to be family. Families survive, and even thrive, as original two-parent units, as single parent households and as new, blended groups. Most families are not the tidy package for which we hope. Most families are like a Christmas package that has been thrown around in the mail, a bit torn and tattered around the edges, with a flat bow that is half on and half off. Family life is messy! But as with that Christmas package, once the gift is opened, what is inside is still in one piece, valuable and wanted!

For us, there is a strong analogy between our family and our home. There are brief periods when the house is sparkling clean, everything is in its place, all odds and ends are picked up and it looks lovely (this usually means company is coming in our household). However, most times there are papers on the table and floor, laundry waiting to be done, splashes on the floor and fingerprints on doors and walls. That's how our family is. There are brief moments when love for the whole family is evident: when everyone pitches in to help a brother or sister move, or when we celebrate a birthday; when a hurt has been addressed and peace once more is attained; when we play or celebrate together. But most times our family is messy—there are misunderstandings and communication is limited to necessary topics, one person doesn't agree with the behavior or habits of another, judgments are made about the choice of career and boyfriend/girlfriend and on and on.

ESTABLISHING RESPONSIBILITY FOR SELF: THE YOUNG ADULT TASK

As we look back through the growing and evolving of our family, it seems like only yesterday that our children were toddlers, following us around with their wonderful innocence and keen curiosity. How did we reach these mid-life years so rapidly? Now our children are stepping off into adulthood, seeking their place in the unknown future.

Eventually the time comes when it is natural and healthy for our children to leave their home and move on with their lives. They need to accept emotional and financial responsibility for themselves. They are in the process of trying to develop intimate peer relationships, preparing to establish themselves in work and attempting to define themselves as adults within their family. These are their tasks as they move into adulthood. For some these tasks will seem daunting. For others, they will be natural, next steps. Young adults who live in single parent or blended households may have coped with very similar challenges earlier in their lives. If they handled the earlier transitions well, the tasks of young adulthood may seem easy in comparison. If these issues, however, were left unresolved, they will need to be faced again and handled in a way that fosters constructive growth as young adults. Sometimes we do not agree with the timing or approach that the young adults in our families choose. We think they are too young or perhaps too immature. Then there are also times, as they enter their late 20's or early 30's, when we wonder if they will ever leave!

Having read about young adult growth and life tasks, we knew what to expect from ourselves and our children. By putting a definition on what we were experiencing, it helped us to realize we were going through normal readjustments, difficult though they be. Knowing there will be crises as well as joy-filled and humorous intervals, we were more receptive to the changes taking place. There are moments when we even feel excited about what the future may hold.

We need to be supportive and encouraging to our children as they face the demands of choosing a job or career, a significant relationship, a place to live, a college to attend or a year or two away to "find" themselves.

As a family, each individual within our family unit will make an adjustment in some way when the first child leaves. This exit from our family system upsets the balance in our home and shifts the roles each of us has assumed. There are many mixed emotions at play—perhaps relief on the part of a younger sibling because he won't be teased any longer, as well as sadness that things are changing. For another, it may be happiness at having a room to herself. Perhaps one of the children will withdraw for awhile because their big brother or sister, who always protected them, is no longer going to be there every day.

For us it is a large bag of mixed emotions. We worry about how our children will behave and with whom they will associate. We are concerned, wondering if they'll be able to make it on their own economically. We have questions about the continuation of their faith. Will church be important to them? Will God be part of their lives? Will they drop out of religious practice for awhile? We are also happy they are moving on with their own lives and excited about the reasons why they are leaving home. We look forward to having more time for ourselves and time with each other.

With this mixed bag of emotions, we have found that we depend a great deal on trust and faith. Trust that we have done the best we could in raising our children, even with all the mistakes we have made. Faith that they will go forward with a sound foundation in God's love and care.

LEAVING HOME—RETURNING HOME

It is important to remember that while children do eventually leave our homes, they do not leave our families or our connectedness with them. Our children are leaving home in various ways. Each child's leaving has been different, just as each birth was different. The first to leave our family was the second of four children. At age 18, we worried a great deal about his maturity and questioned his readiness to leave the "nest". When we were 18, we thought we could take on the world. When our child was 18, we were delighted he could tie his shoelaces! We questioned how this child would ever be able to make it on his own. What we were really trying to deal with was whether we could let go! There is purpose, satisfaction, self-worth and joy in our role as parents. When our child left, there was emptiness, fear, anxiety and confusion. Parenting the other three children was different without this child's interaction. How would we get along without his spontaneity, humor and constant challenges to keep us honest?

His mother wept and wept, and kept telling herself she was foolish. He wouldn't be that far away, only in the next state. She could talk to him by phone. None of these rational thoughts helped. His father wished him well and said very little about his leaving, although there were tears in his eyes as he hugged him goodbye. What we were dealing with was a loss—the loss of a "comfortable" role as parents and an uncertainty about what would happen, not only to our child, but to ourselves and the rest of our family now that he was gone.

On the other hand, our eldest son was very comfortable living at home. He was not the least bit demanding. He took care of his own laundry, did some cooking and cleaned his own room. He shoveled snow and cut the grass in the summer. He attended a local college and wanted to live at home during this time. He was the third child to leave home physically and yet had emotionally left a number of years prior to his departure. He was respectful of our interactions, although we almost had to make appointments with him to catch him when he was at home. He was always considerate of those in the household, but he pretty much went his own way.

Our reaction to his moving out of our home was very different than with our other children. He was older, in his mid 20's and had more lived experience. We had less fear and anxiety, more confidence in his ability to be independent. We missed his companionship, his presence in our home. We also missed his talent of being able to fix anything that was broken! At the time he left, we were also more aware of the need to grieve his leaving and were able to talk about how we were feeling. This helped to make his departure less stressful.

When all except our last child had moved on, a new dynamic was created, that of having an only-child household. Our daughter tried to assume the roles that our other children had played in the family system and things became pretty chaotic for awhile. She was the center of all the parenting that once was spread around and this became burdensome for her. Without even realizing what was happening, we found ourselves "tightening" the reins. We began treating her like an early adolescent rather than encouraging her development as a young adult. It took time and others' observations to trust enough to let her travel the path to adulthood. She carried a double burden. She was the last at home and also a female. It seems we had a double standard when it came to the freedoms allowed our children. The males in our family were allowed more latitude. We have more fear and a need for more control of our daughter's security, safety and future.

Just when we think we've adjusted to the changes in the household, a surprise pops up to give us another opportunity to be flexible! One or more of the children may decide to return. Because of an economic situation, a graduation from school, a change in or lack of a job or dozens of other reasons, it may be necessary for them to live at home again. This means everyone shifts again as we all seek to find a mutual level of relating to each other. This child who has returned is an adult. They have experienced their independence and freedom, making choices that did not have a direct impact on the living situation of the family. A clear verbalization of expectations on the part of all family members makes this time together more fruitful. However it may take some pushing and pulling to have this happen.

The first child to leave our home was also the first to return. It took us months to renegotiate the rules and each other's expectations. Although we had no curfew for when our son was to be home, we went back and forth about his calling if he was not coming home at all. Having been on his own, he had some trouble understanding why he needed to call us. Once we explained that we were concerned and worried if we found his bed empty, he agreed to this understanding. We didn't relish those early morning phone calls, but we did appreciate them. We do not seem to have a preventive mentality in our society. We react more often than we respond, so it isn't unusual to face some conflict and disagreement over some rules that we wish to establish for these re-entries. Renegotiation of our relationship with our son meant our listening to and observing him with a new attitude. We recognize the changes we saw. His room was clean and neat, he had a responsible job and handled situations when he was on his own which he told us about at various times. As a result of this, our respect for him grew and eased the transition of no longer seeing him as a child.

Another issue attached to leaving home that we looked at within ourselves was the expectation for our children to live out the goals and dreams we had for ourselves that have not come into being. Helping our children establish their own lives means giving them the freedom to pursue their own goals and dreams, as they form them, without the lingering shadows of their parents' unfulfilled desires.

We want to avoid the two extremes that can happen during this stage of the family life cycle. As our children become adults, we can hold onto them too tightly or totally let them go. We want to work toward a mid-point of releasing our children with our blessings as they move on to adulthood.

One of the ways of totally letting them go is by expecting them to be the ones to initiate contact with us once they leave home. This can be done with the best of intentions by thinking they need time to adjust to being gone from the household or by not wanting to interfere with their lives. However, we need to strive for the balance of being interested in them, wanting to be part of their lives while at the same time not being overbearing or intrusive. We needed to discuss with them how much contact is too much or too little. Calling or writing to just say hello or to let them know we have been thinking of them is one way we remain connected.

If the only time we contact them is when there is a problem or when we want to put our two cents worth into what they are doing, then they certainly will not look forward to our calls or letters nor will they be well received. An overdependency on our children may occur when our marriage relationship falters or does not measure up to what we think it should. When our need for closeness, intimacy, dependability, trust and commitment are not met with our spouse, we may unconsciously turn to our children to have these needs fulfilled. We often are not even aware that this is happening until they prepare to depart from the family.

RELATING TO OUR YOUNG ADULT CHILDREN

There are things we can do to help us relate to our children as adults. The first seems so obvious, yet is most often what we don't consciously do. It is to recognize and accept the fact that our little sons and daughters have become adults. As we watch them struggle, make mistakes, behave in ways of which we may not approve, it is so hard to realize we cannot control them. Control is a very large issue because we want our children to go where we want them to go! When they take off on an entirely different path, we are left wondering where we went wrong. We thought we had aimed them in the right direction, we gave them the best we had and yet, they aren't "landing" where we planned.

Our eldest son studied engineering and laser optics. He has a keen mind and the ability to translate his thoughts to his hands. During his college years, thoughts of where he would go to do his graduate work and where he would eventually establish his career went through our minds. When he told us he wasn't happy in his chosen courses and wanted to be a parts manager we were very surprised. Would all of his intelligence and talent be wasted? His mother reacted with extremely judgmental thoughts regarding parts managers! After many discussions and lots of reflection on her unfounded judgments, she went to him and apologized for her outburst and told him it didn't matter what field of work he chose, as long as he enjoyed it and found value in what he did. His father did not have the same reaction as mother to this news. In fact, he was pleased that his son had found something he really liked.

We had to admit we do not have control over anyone's lives but our own. We try to rest in the belief that our children are not our possessions, only loaned to us by God to guide and encourage with an optimistic spirit. Then we can go about the work of changing ourselves in order that we may relate to them in an adult-to-adult manner.

One way we have done this is by looking at how we offer our children hospitality. When we speak or visit, is it done with respect for their ideas and opinions whether we agree or not? Are we able to speak with them about their choices in ways we would speak with our closest friends—with an open mind and freedom to be ourselves with each other?

When one of our other sons made a life style choice with which we did not agree, we felt as though we had been slapped in the face. We thought our values had been completely rejected. However, after much reflection and discussion between ourselves and our son, we were able to keep the door open to him. We stated our objections, the reasons for our concern, but also told him how much we loved him and that he was always welcome in our home. We did not cut ourselves off from him. We saw and spoke regularly with each other. The time came, when he decided this choice he had made was no longer one he wanted to pursue. We comforted and supported him through our discussions and affection until he worked through this crisis time in his life. In this instance, all worked out the way we had hoped.

Then there are those times when our desire for a particular outcome is not brought to fruition. We still need to maintain an "open door" policy. It has been through a choice one of other our children made that we have learned, once again, how to let go of our need to control. Since this child's choice is not one we would have made, we have had to look long and hard at our attitude of believing we know what is best for our children. Do we really know that? Are we attempting to play God with their lives? We have had to look at our prejudices, our materialistic tendencies, and remember our fundamental belief that God is also active in this family in order to let go of our righteous attitude that we know what is best.

We have sought to find ways to show our children that we value who they are. We have asked their opinions in making decisions about our own lives and have turned to them for their advice, comfort and input. This is a mutual path we are now walking and we parents are not the only ones with "pearls of wisdom." They have their own "pearls of wisdom" to extend to us. These insights have often kept us honest about who we are ourselves. Their observations about us are usually pretty much on target! It is also helpful at these times to verbally tell our children that we are trying to create a different way of interacting with them as adults and ask for their help and cooperation in doing this. When we find ourselves reverting to our old way of attempting to run things—telling them what they should be doing—we can catch ourselves and admit that, "Here we go again, treating you as if you are 10 years old. Let's begin this conversation again."

Very often our children's behavior can "hook" us and we immediately become entangled as parent and child. The way one of our children handled money was a "grabber" for us. We heard ourselves saying, "You want to be treated as an adult, have the freedom adults have, yet you still are in debt over your head!" We would then continue the pattern of bailing our child out of the difficulty, not addressing this issue until finances once again became a problem. Once we were able to specifically name the behaviors that drove us crazy, we could then change our reaction to the situation. We no longer come to our child's rescue when in debt. Instead, we encourage the establishment of a budget and make suggestions as to ways money can be saved. We'll know we have accomplished our task of treating this child as an adult when we stop making suggestions unless they are requested! We're still working on this. A sense of humor during this transition time is invaluable. We are going to make mistakes, we are going to be frustrated, and it will be necessary to laugh at ourselves and our attempts at fashioning this different relationship with our children.

RELATING TO OUR PARENTS AS ADULTS

In attempting to cross the bridge of seeing our children as adults, it was helpful for us to be aware of the unfinished work that needed to be done in our own family of origin. If we at times are not treated as adults by our own parents, then we do not have an adequate role model to follow with our own children. So it is possible that, at the same time we are establishing an adult-to-adult relationship with our children, we are also trying to become that adult child in the eyes of our own parents.

If there are left over issues, we can address them either through writing, journaling, or verbalizing them. This can help to clarify the relationship we had with our parents, and we can also recognize that this parent/child relationship is seldom all bad or all good. It helps us to have a balanced perspective on our own upbringing and can even begin an investigation for information about who our parents were as persons, not just as parents.

We spoke with relatives to hear their stories about our mother or father. By speaking with our brothers and sisters or aunts and uncles, we began to realize everyone has their own perspective of our parents. By putting all of this information together, we have a more accurate picture of our own father and mother.

Establishing adult-to-adult relationships with our own parents is not easy work. For some reason we fear upsetting our parents or making them angry. Therefore we either avoid them or become like children again when we are with them. In order to change this, we have attended workshops and spoken with counselors as we became aware of the things that made us feel like children when we were with our parents. They weren't major issues but little things that would cast us back in time in a split second. Perhaps a tone of voice, a critical statement that we'd heard over and over again, a cynical remark that only we knew what was meant. Slowly and cautiously, we began to make changes in the way we responded at these times. We became honest with ourselves about how their comments made us feel. We also verbalize our thoughts to them in as kindly a way as possible, rather than leaving their presence with pent up anger and frustration.

We firmly believe that our parents did the best they could with the experience, education and skills they possess. We do not reflect on our family of origin to place any blame for why our life is as it is. The reflection is done to increase our understanding of our family history and to become aware of the traditions, attitudes and behaviors we wish to continue as well as to see more clearly the areas we wish to change. The benefit derived from putting energy and time into looking at past generations is that it offers us choices for how we now wish to determine our own lives.

We often either repeat the patterns of relationships that existed in our families of origin, or we rebel against them. By reflecting on our family of origin, we can see factually what has happened in the past and now make a conscious decision to continue the previous pattern or make a change within our present family. This has been a very freeing exercise for us and one that has been of great assistance as we try to deal with our own children as adults. By remembering how we felt and what we experienced as we were going through this transition of adolescence to adulthood, we can better understand our own children as they go through this same process.

HOME ALONE—OUR RELATIONSHIP AS A COUPLE

The biggest adjustment for us right now is realizing the two of us are alone in our home. At times it is strange and stressful and other times it is freeing and wonderful. We now have time to reflect on who we are at this age, what goals and dreams have been attained, what our hopes and fears are for the future and what marriage and family means now that our children are leaving our household.

A danger at this stage of our lives can be that an overdependency on our children may occur when our marriage relationship falters or does not measure up to what we think it should. When our need for closeness, intimacy, dependability, trust and commitment are not met with our spouse, we may unconsciously turn to our children to have these needs fulfilled. We often are not even aware that this is happening until they prepare to depart from the family.

Fortunately we have spent time over the years working on our relationship. We made a decision about ten years into our marriage that our first priority would be just that—our relationship. This was as a result of some harried times, feelings of being taken for granted, being in a rut and thinking there had to be more to this marriage bond then what we were experiencing. It was a decision both of us had to make in order for it to work. It probably has been one of the best decisions either of us has made. We made the time to have fun together. We took dancing lessons and spent many days at a ski slope, even though one of us never did get the hang of it! We would go together—one to ski, the other to read in the lodge or take wonderful walks in the woods. We taught religious education and quickly discovered teaching eighth graders was not one of our gifts or talents! We were active on our parish council. We made a marriage encounter weekend and have participated in workshops to stimulate our relationship. When necessary, we would have breakfast out to discuss issues without interruption. Some of these opportunities presented themselves through the invitation of friends and acquaintances, some through our desire to learn more about our religion, and some just because they were fun. We also searched for some of these experiences because over the course of our years together as husband and wife, we found ourselves restless and discontent with our marriage. We needed to somehow create a newness and freshness in our relationship. We refer to these times as our spring or fall "tune-up."

Each time a new job offer came along or a decision as to how many activities each of our children would participate in, or an extended family crisis arose, we based our answers and behavior on the priority of our relationship. It wasn't always a delightful, care-free choice, but it gave us a concrete value base from which our decisions were made.

We have found the qualities that first attracted us to each other still exist. They sometimes become hidden under layers of stress, of years of not noticing these qualities, or focusing on their extremes. But they are still there and worth uncovering. In fact, now that we are alone in our home, we are discovering things about each other that we've never been aware of before.

Dealing with change is never easy. However, moving through these times can be a source of discovery and relief. A friend of ours who is divorced has shared with us what it has been like for her, as she too, experiences the ups and downs of relating to her children as adults. It has been important for her not to get caught in the middle of the relationship they each are trying to establish with their father, her ex-spouse. It is not easy to listen to the frustrations, and at times, disappointments they are feeling as a result of their expectations of their father. However, she has found that by listening to them, and not stepping in to rescue them, that a smoother, more realistic and meaningful relationship is in the process of development. She is discovering attributes in her children that she has not recognized until now.

She is relieved not to have to deal any longer with questions of with whom will the children live, who will carry health insurance for them and which parent will be contacted by schools. Her relationship with her ex-spouse is smoother now that their children are grown. She has been able to put closure on the issues that created the stress and tension between them and now is beginning a new chapter in her life free from bitterness and anger. If we can commit ourselves to what is important to us—our love for our family—we can accept change with its pain and disruption because it also helps us to find surprises and strengths within ourselves that we weren't aware we possessed.

CHOOSING TO BE MARRIED

A very obvious change in family occurs when our children marry. This time can provide a common ground on which we can meet as adults. Marriage is a time of joy and anticipation but also a time of stress, for our children and ourselves as parents. How involved do we become? How do we show we are interested and care without interfering?

Getting to know our sons or daughters-in-law can be like a game of cat and mouse. All parties concerned put their best foot forward. There are questions we want to ask, but fear being seen as a busy-body or nagging mother/father-in-law. Our children see their spouses differently than we do. Their concern is someone to love and care for them, someone whom they can love and cherish. Our concern is our own child's well being. Will this new person make him/her feel special? Will they help them to mature and grow as persons? Will they be a spiritual partner, helping their faith to increase? Will they recognize and respect their gifts, talents and beliefs? We voiced these concerns to our children and hoped they would reflect upon them. We then needed to let them make their own decisions, no matter if we thought they were right or wrong.

A number of people did not rejoice over our marriage 30 years ago. These people were people who loved us and wanted only the best for us. Their opinion was that we were not a good match. We have proven that their opinion was just that—their opinion. This experience of ours has often helped us to step back and remember that we do not know what the future will hold for our children or whom the right person is for them to share their lives.

During the time of preparation for marriage, we offered our children the gift of an Engaged Encounter weekend. Gift means no strings attached so they were free to accept or decline this invitation. One accepted, one declined. As the planning for the weddings continued, we tried to remember this was their wedding day, not ours. When our advice was sought, we gave it and when it was not, we kept quiet. A wise parent sometimes knows when to speak and when to remain mute!

Once our children married, our relationship with them shifted again to include their spouses. They now have another family, their in-laws, who need to be considered. Just the question of where holidays, birthdays and anniversaries will be spent is often a source of conflict for all involved. We need to call on our parental generosity by not making demands that cause undue stress on the relationship they are establishing as newlymarrieds.

This is especially difficult when family traditions have been carried on for generations. From the very beginning of our marriage, we have spent every Christmas at Ken's parents' home. There was never a year that the whole family didn't gather for a full course meal, the opening of gifts and the company of each other.

Since our children were the first grandchildren in our family to marry, we were the ones who broke this tradition. They spend Christmas with their wives' families now, since Thanksgiving is spent with us. This was difficult for some of our extended family to understand, though they did accept this change. During the first year of our son's marriage, he tried to be at his in-laws as well as stopping at his grandparents. Since some distance is involved, this was not a simple or satisfactory solution. He was not able to relax and enjoy his in-laws because he knew he had to get on the road before it got too late. We talked about other ways we could compromise on this, and now they visit their grandparents at another time during the Christmas season.

Our responsibility as parents also changes once our children marry. Our other married son has enjoyed the sport of auto racing for many years. He started by helping out as a "gofer" for a racing team and just a few years ago realized his dream to be a driver. While attending a race in Canada with him and his wife, we were watching him when another car hit his and he went into a wall. After he climbed out of the car, it was obvious that he had jarred his neck and it was quite painful. As we started to go to him to suggest he get some medical attention, we saw his wife running over to him. At that moment, we stopped in our tracks. We realized it was his wife who needed to talk to him and suggest he get assistance, not his parents. We believe this was a moment of grace, to see so clearly we are no longer his primary support. Just as his mom and dad are first in each other's lives, his wife must be first in his. This is not a displacement of us as his parents. It is a natural, healthy change that results when our children choose to marry.

As we go through this dance of holding on and letting go of our children, we find it helpful for us to look at how we left our own families. Was it a happy leave taking? Did we leave with everyone's good wishes and agreement? Or were there tensions and conflict around our moving out of our original households? By checking back to look at the emotional, physical and spiritual issues surrounding that time in our own lives, it gave us some clues as to how we are handling our children's leaving.

Jerrie was an emotional support to her mother when we married and left a void when she moved out of her household. We looked to see if we were re-living that dependency with one of our own children. Ken was the one to whom his family turned in crisis. He helped smooth the way in solving problems in his family. We questioned if we look to one of our children to fill that place in our life. By realizing what roles we played in our own families, we can now see if we are expecting the same from our children. In looking back, we gained some insight to help us work through the tasks needed at this time of transition.

CARING FOR OUR PARENTS

Our generation has been called the sandwich generation because we are raising children and caring for our own parents at the same time. It can be like a chocolate cream cookie, at times very sweet and tasty and other times feeling squeezed, like the white filling, until you think you will crumble. Just when our children are starting to become less dependent, our parents are looking to us for more assistance. How much assistance depends on their health, their economic status, the loss of their friends and their support network. As Jerrie's mother's health deteriorated, it became necessary to assist her in finding services that would enable her to remain independent as long as possible. Medical care, home assistance and transportation were all factors that need to be considered or put into place.

We need to learn how to be supportive of our parents without overfunctioning for them. This can be a very fine line as they work through the process of aging. Retirement is experienced differently by Ken's mom and dad. Once again, there is a shift in their relationship. Ken's dad had to deal with issues of self-esteem since he no longer was working, and a great deal of worth is found in having a job. There were the losses of relationships that were work connected and he had to answer the question of "what do I do now?" His mom had to adjust to having dad home more, interrupting her routine, and she too felt the loss of social contacts through his job. We, who are the middle generation, need to listen to their concerns and frustrations but not get caught in between them. We can help them turn to each other as they grapple with this change in their lives. Once again, honest communication becomes key to a balanced adjustment.

It is helpful for us to have a clear understanding of the boundaries of our own lives. How much involvement, energy and time, both psychic and physical, can be given to our children and parents before the stress becomes too great and we crumble? This varies depending on the circumstances we are experiencing, such as job change, unemployment, increase or loss in economic status, health, cultural dictates, etc. Once we are consciously aware of what we are willing and not willing to do, we then need to be very clear in communicating this to our children and parents.

If and when the time comes when our parents are not able to physically remain independent, we then need to look at what alternatives and options are available. This process is one that involves not only ourselves, but also our immediate family and other siblings.

What is required to resolve some of these issues is for our parent(s) to accept their strengths and limitations and for us to take responsibility for what we can appropriately do. Recognizing that we are not able to bring Jerrie's mother into our home, even though we know this is what is desired, has created a spiritual and emotional battle within us. We constantly question what is the Christian and loving thing to do. We don't want to hurt her and we know with all our hearts that we love her, and yet we also know we are not capable, at this present time, of having her with us. We question if we are being selfish, if we're putting our own wants and needs before hers. After much prayer, soul searching and consultation, we came to the decision that the circumstances in our life right now prevent us from inviting her into our home. We feel a great sadness knowing we have disappointed her and sincerely wish circumstances were different. Having Jerrie's brothers' support through this decision making process has been a great help.

Even though we are at peace with our decision, this has not meant that her mother has accepted this fact. What we are dealing with are her expectations of Jerrie as her daughter and, just as we have to give our children the freedom from our expectations of them, we have to have the freedom not to live up to our own parents' expectations of us.

We need to be patient with ourselves and with them. We sometimes feel pressured and stressed by thinking we have to meet all their needs. It is when we think we have to do it all ourselves that we lose the sense of balance in our life. If we are stressed, pulled in many directions, trying to keep everyone happy (parents, spouse, children), we will be the losers. We will feel resentful and angry. We then lash out at those we love the most. The toll it takes is our own emotional, physical and spiritual well-being.

We have accepted the reality that we most likely will not meet all of our parents' expectations. We can, however, support them in ways that show our love and hope these will be accepted as given. We can let them know the many ways they have given to us over the years for which we are grateful—the way they listened to us, the way they nursed and comforted us when sick or hurt, the playful times when we laughed over silly things, the emotional and material support over the years, the skills that allow us to fix and create things, and especially the values they have instilled in us.

Once we recognized and reflected on all that our parents have given to us and done for us, we acknowledged what a blessing they have been in our lives. We all like to hear what we've done—what legacy we are leaving to those who follow us.

Since Jerrie's mother lives a great distance from us, the way we have communicated most frequently has been by mail. This has afforded Jerrie the opportunity to put in writing how much she appreciates the way she raised her. She could express her thanks by specifically stating the things she remembered over the years.

Our parents continue to give us the gift of our history. A special moment was when Ken's dad was in the hospital and through some questions about his life—great-grandparents, his childhood—we learned to see he had joys and struggles just as we have. This "story-telling" created a bonding between us and helped him to reflect on the life he has lived. As our parents tell us about their lives in ways that are new to us, it is a good time to ask them how they felt when we left home. We may be surprised to learn they experienced the same struggles and joys we are now experiencing as our own children leave our household.

Our parents are the glue that keeps the family in touch. They carry on traditions that bring us together to celebrate our being family. They help us to pause in this hectic time of life and re-evaluate what is really important. They enable us to have a different perspective on ourselves and our siblings.

If we work at it, instead of being a sandwich, we can be a bridge for three generations. Very often our own parents talk to their grandchildren in ways we cannot. They are their cheerleaders and confidants. Their grandparents become their advocates by providing non-judgmental physical, spiritual and emotional assistance. They are keepers of the light on our journey toward God, who then passes that light onto us in hopes we can do the same.

We have found that the key for us in trying to maintain and enrich the relationship with our children and our parents is in knowing our own strengths and limitations. Each change that takes place in the lives of all our family members creates new stresses and new opportunities. Our attitudes determine how we respond to these shifting interactions. If we have the attitude that their approaches to us are an intrusion into our lives, we will spend these years in constant turmoil with feelings of annoyance and anger. If we determine our behaviors by these attitudes and feelings, we will be more likely to cut ourselves off from our family.

If, however, the boundaries we establish for our own lives are elastic enough—adjustable—we can maintain a semblance of balance for ourselves while staying connected to all the generations of our family. We cannot honestly say we have established these flexible boundaries. What we can say is we are aware of our need to do so and are continually working on it. Sometimes we are better at it than at other times. We are learning more about ourselves as we go through each event, illness, marriage and leave-taking.

We have learned to be patient with ourselves, as we stumble, fall, pick ourselves up and try again. We regret the times we haven't handled situations with our children or parents in ways that could have shown more care and love. We are thankful for the times when we have responded to them with compassion and understanding. We look forward to the opportunities that will come and know that, even though we may mess it up more than once in the future, we will always be family!

3

SHARING FAITH
WITH YOUNG ADULTS

OUR FAITH JOURNEY

What is faith to us? It is trusting and believing in God who gives us the energy and ability to live our lives in hope. When we were expecting our first child, we trusted that God would provide what we needed. We had no money, we were physically separated because of a military call up and we were living with Jerrie's parents, but we had faith that not only would we survive, but that a new world would be opened to us. We both looked forward to this child although he was not planned, and our greatest hope was that we could be together for his birth.

And we were! Experiences like that not only define but sustain our faith.

We live our faith each and every day. We stay connected to God by praying, by talking with each other about the ways we recognize God's action in our life and being an active part of a community of people who value their faith as we do. We experience the peaks and valleys of our own lives and relate to people how these daily events put us in touch with the death and resurrection of Jesus. Our faith gives us the courage to work through the difficult times we all experience as a family and to enjoy and celebrate the happy times we share. It is important to us that we pass on the value of our faith to our children as they become adults.

As we think about ways to accomplish this, we look at our own faith to see why it is important to us. So often we assume values by osmosis. Certain values were instilled in us by our parents, and we continue to carry them without examining whether or not they are what we want for ourselves. Do they really fit who we are now?

When our children were younger, we decided we needed some time for ourselves to just get away. We came across a brochure that advertised a couple-directed retreat, and after asking a brother and his wife to baby-sit, off we went. It was while we were on this retreat that for the first time, we really examined the religion in which we had been raised.

We are the children of three Catholic parents and one Methodist father. Both of us were born and raised as Roman Catholics. We asked ourselves that weekend whether or not we chose to remain in this particular denomination, and by the time we left, we had made a conscious decision to continue to be Roman Catholics. Our reasons for deciding this were many. We receive strength and fortitude through the sacraments and the Eucharistic liturgy which constantly reminds us of God's redeeming power. We look to the teachings of our Church to help us make decisions based on our own conscience, and we are also grateful that our Church is in the forefront, both in speaking out for and acting on behalf of social justice.

It was a very satisfying and fulfilling exercise to make an adult decision to be Roman Catholic. Our Church provides many challenges which motivate us to seek and search for ways that lead us closer to God.

This search is never ending. Just as our children were growing up, so too did we need to continue our psychological and spiritual development. We are still learning, experiencing and expanding our images of God. At one time, we judged the "level" of our faith by our feelings of closeness to God and compared ourselves to other people whom we thought were holier or closer to our Creator than were we, but it was too frustrating. Like comparing yourself as a parent to someone you perceive to "have it all together," it was depressing and self-defeating. We have since learned to be our own judge of our faith-fulness.

As we were raising our children, we often questioned ourselves about their religious education. Because they went to public elementary schools we wondered whether or not they were learning enough about God. Their mother had 12 years of Catholic education and their father went to public schools with one hour weekly of "released time" religious education, so we brought two very diverse experiences to the faith development of ourselves and our family. We weren't aware at this time that we were our children's primary educators, and we looked to the church to give them a solid foundation in faith.

In hindsight, we realize that we were the ones who gave them their foundation, just as our parents gave us ours, supported by the church and extended family and friends. If what they learned in school is not lived out at home, then it's on shifting sands that our children build their faith.

Could we have done more to share our faith? Certainly. Did we know that then? Certainly not! We did the best we could, just as our parents did their best for us. We could have been kinder and more compassionate, and spent more time listening to our children and understanding their fears, concerns and questions. But that does not negate how we witnessed to our love of God through our love for them. We gave what we had, what we understood through our experience at that time.

JOHN AND KATHY'S FAITH JOURNEY

Friends of ours, both in a second marriage, have two daughters who lived with their biological mother until one went to college and the other was a senior in high school. Their stepmother, Kathy, has made a priority of making their "new" unit a family. It has taken sacrifice, patience, lots of communication and contact with John's ex-wife to realize this goal. It meant listening to John's anger, hurt and bitterness over his divorce. It meant that John and Kathy had to work out between them who was best able to make arrangements for the girls' visitations, who was able to handle the request for increased child support AND find ways to keep their own relationship healthy.

Because the four of them had only summers, weekends and holidays to be together, they often found themselves walking on eggshells with each other. Simple arguments that would have been let go in a family living together day-to-day got blown out of proportion. Everything was taken much too seriously and personally. Somehow, they had to make up for the early, daily experiences of family life that they had missed by not being together then. This was complicated by the fact that the girls' faith and beliefs had been formed by many experiences, including a number of stepfathers and their biological father's remarriage.

How do they share faith, traditions and values? In the words of John and Kathy,

> Children do not come with a rule book. We don't know if what we do is right or wrong. You parent by the seat of your pants and shoot from the hip. It really is a great leap of faith! Our children are in their 20's, no longer children but adults. As children, their view of their Catholic faith was that it was external; it was what you

'had to do.' To them, it was more social than spiritual, so it seemed 'fake.' It didn't really mean anything to them.

Today they watch us live our faith every day. Now that we 'do' church every day, it has taken on a whole new meaning, an internal, personal, spiritual meaning. It's beginning to make more sense and as it does, it begins to become more important. Our daughters tell us they trust us and have faith in us because we back up what we say with what we do. We don't push religion on them, but we show them by what we do every day and that has a positive effect on their lives and their own faith formation, as well as ours. God is not real because we say so but because they see him in our lives every day. Faith comes in steps. Formation of faith does not happen overnight but has to be cultivated like a garden. You plant the seed, tend the soil, water it when there is no rain, but most importantly you position the plants where they can see the sun and grow to their maximum potential. So it is with the seedling we call children, the immature plant we call adolescence and the young and tender adult. Family is the same thing, always growing, needing constant tending, constant nurturing.

The expectation in John and Kathy's household is that each person is respected and everyone needs to speak up. John commented on how they have become closer to the children now that they are adults. As teens there were many arguments, but now he sees their children as contemporaries. They enjoy their children's company and do not hesitate to praise them and tell them how proud they are of them.

A controversial issue in their household is living together before marriage. Marriage and commitment are a big topic for them since so many of the girls' experiences have dealt with divorce. Each may see things differently, but they listen to each other's opinions, each making a case for their beliefs. Their love of each other is not based on agreement but respect.

Recently, Kathy became a Catholic. Although raised as a Mormon, her grandparents took her to Mass as a child, and

Kathy remembers the peace and hope she felt at those times. When she told her family, the girls were thrilled that they would now share the same religion. As a result of Kathy's decision, their daughters made their confirmation and the discussions concerning the Catholic faith were enriched by the fact that the three of them were studying at the same time.

John got drawn into this and after having been away from church for a number of years started sharing Sunday Mass with his family. What a great celebration they had the day Kathy was baptized, received the Eucharist, was confirmed and had her marriage blessed! Is it any wonder these sacraments hold a great deal of importance and meaning in their family?

ENCOURAGING THE FAITH OF YOUNG ADULTS

Traditionally, the late teens and early twenties is a time for questioning one's religious traditions and beliefs. Young people are disengaging from their parent's family and establishing their own adult lives. Part of this involves forming their own patterns of faith and belief that speak to their needs as they begin to take their own faith seriously. Some do it by dropping out of the traditional church completely; others explore a wide variety of often offbeat cult and religious forms; others may just take a step back and examine their beliefs more closely.

Somewhere in the later teen years, a son or daughter will come to the dinner table and say something like "Mom, I don't know if I believe in God any more!" or, "Dad, I don't think I'll be going to church with you for a while. I've got to work some things out *for myself.*"

As parents, we react in a variety of ways. Too often, we express shock; we feel we've failed as parents, when we should rejoice, because our "child" is beginning to grow up. Our children are not only beginning to deal with choices of work, lifestyle and values, but are also beginning to *take charge* of their own faith growth. Taking responsibility for one's own life and asking questions about life's ultimate meaning is not always easy. It involves doubting, struggling with new concepts and even sometimes *rejecting* traditional assumptions, but it is an important *and necessary* step for maturing faith.

It is unfortunate that so many parents and church ministers view the questioning as "losing one's faith" rather than the positive affirmation of a person who is truly taking charge of her or his faith life and seeking answers that will provide the fullest possible dimension of a meaningful personal faith.

The community of faith that nurtures and encourages individual expressions of personal faith, *even when they may digress from our own faith,* must be affirmed. The family and community of faith that encourages such spiritual growth is being faithful to the young adult quest: searching for a faith which will have true meaning for their lives. For some, this may include rejecting some earlier training or traditional concepts, which many have viewed negatively. However, the resulting positive spiritual development makes it worth the effort.

Parents can support faith growth at this important time by actively encouraging religious growth and involvement through family or one-on-one discussions and through their personal witness as people of faith. Parents can also support and involve young adults in relationships, faith communities and programs and activities in parish life, college campus ministries or movements which help them deepen their faith life.

These involvements can help the young adult by (1) focusing on his or her continued identity and intimacy needs; (2) presenting a clear and compelling understanding of faith which speaks to their experience as young adults; (3) challenging young adults to take responsibility for their own faith lives; (4) providing expressions for worship and prayer which nurture the growing awareness of God's presence in their lives; (5) stimulating challenging discussions and the sharing of faith stories which express growing responsibility for their faith lives; (6) providing opportunities for involvement and participation in various faith communities; (7) exhibiting models of mature faith personally in adults, and in films, books and speakers; (8) engaging them in examining social justice and actively responding to the needs of others through service; (9) offering opportunities to be involved in prayer groups and Scripture study groups; and (10) providing retreat experiences which include faith sharing, prayer, Scripture, faith reflection and worship in a setting in which mature faith can grow. As parents, we should support their involvement in communities and programs which strengthen their identity, foster relationships with other young adults, explore meaning questions and offer service opportunities.

Now we want to share with you some of the ways that we have tried to share faith with our young adult children. We do this to encourage you to continue parenting for faith growth as your child becomes a young adult, not to try to tell you what to do.

THROUGH THE GOSPEL OF FAMILY LIFE

Each time we dried our children's tears, held them when they had nightmares, changed their diapers, took them to church, read them bible stories, taught them how to bless themselves and say their prayers, mopped up their spilled milk or searched for them with all our neighbors when they ran away from home as preschoolers, all of these times we loved them.

As they became teenagers, they tested us harder and more frequently, rejected our values, searched for a place to belong, tried their wings and fell flat on their faces. We spent hours discussing why they had to go to church as long as they lived in our home, answering their questions about their sexuality, arguing over the rules and regulations of the house, talking about drugs, helping them sort through Christian service projects for Confirmation, even questioning if they wanted to be confirmed and wondering if they really understood their committment in the acceptance of this sacrament (naturally mother thought she was the judge and jury with this one!).

We walked the floors or lay in bed tossing and turning, late nights and early mornings, waiting to hear the car in the driveway, yelled at them for not calling to let us know where they were, picked one of them up when the police called, questioned the tradition of having parties in local motels after the proms, and basically, through it all, tried to help our children see that they needed to treat themselves and others with dignity and respect. We spoke of the Church's teachings and tried to explain to them that the Church was not an ogre who only told them what NOT to do, but that there is wisdom, reason and cause for its doctrine and teachings.

A hard thing for us as parents to accept is that we cannot "give" faith to anyone, including our children. We can only live it ourselves and try to instill an openness in our children so that they can respond to God's love and God's gift of faith.

Parenting requires a choice on our part. We can think we control our children and hold onto our expectations for them, or we can work at letting go of our need to control and love them because they are God's creations, allowing each to work out their own faith journey. We each must follow our own path.

It is hard, though, because we want them to know and experience the comfort, solace, support, peace, joy and challenge that our faith and Church have given to us, as individuals, as a couple and as parents. It helped us, so we hope it will help them. We want them to know they are never alone or adrift if they have Jesus as their friend, God as their lover and the Holy Spirit as their spiritual connection or energy! We expect them to be church-connected so they will always have a community to help and support them. We expect them to learn more about their faith through adult education, weekend experiences, friends who believe as they do. We believe they need to grow and learn spiritually and can do this by becoming aware of Catholic teaching and tradition. We want to balance the messages that bombard our children from TV and magazines ("Me first," "Thin is beautiful," "More is better," "Sex sells," and "Money means success") with the

Christian message of the new covenant, Jesus and the meaning of the Good News.

As young adults, they began to critically reflect on the beliefs and values that they formed when they were younger. This age brings a new quality of responsibility for one's self and one's choices, particularly ideology and lifestyle. We hope our children will be spiritually aware as they make their lifestyle choices; it opens the way for more critically self-aware commitments in relationships and work.

Part of the reluctance we have in letting go of them is our fear of the unknown. What will support and encourage our children if not what we have known? But if we truly believe that our children are not our possessions and if we believe God loves them and yearns to bring them goodness and life, then we can work at letting go of our control, demands and expectations of them. This ability to let go rests in the basic belief that God is always with us and with our children, and that they will be guided as we have been if they remain open to the moments of grace which are given each day.

Being a parent, time and time again puts us in touch with our own weakness, our sinfulness and our need for forgiveness. It has been our own sense of limitations as parents that has forced us to realize that we need a deeper well to draw from, an inexhaustible source. It has been the times when we have felt most vulnerable and powerless, the times we didn't have the strength we thought we needed to continue to nurture them, the times when we were starving for intimacy and acceptance of ourselves, that we have experienced the love and care of God.

We can let go of our expectations when we remember it has been in these weak moments that God has been most present. By trying to protect our children from experiencing these same weak moments, we are blocking the active work of God through the Holy Spirit in our children's lives.

THROUGH ROLE MODELS OF FAITH

Faith is relational, as expressed to us in the Trinity. We know it is the relationship we continue to have with our adult children that will enable us to express our faith to them whether they live at home, across town or across the country. Since it is how we live our faith that shows our children how important this is, we have spent time thinking about how our parents lived their faith.

Our parents showed us an unswerving faith. They did and continue to do this in many ways:

- through both our mothers' devotion to the Blessed Mother which kept us, as teenagers, on the straight and narrow;

- through novenas, rosaries, Masses for our family members who have died;

- through the strength and courage they showed us at the time of their own children's deaths, even though their loss was great and the pain still present.

They didn't turn away from their God but moved closer toward God's redemption:

- through Ken's parents' love and support of his sisters who divorced and especially through the stability they offered to their grandchildren during these difficult times;

- through our parents' giving of their time, money and talents to their parents and siblings, to neighbors, to teens who had no one else to talk to, and to the community;

- through prayer, that was observed daily as Jerrie watched her father on his knees beside his bed each morning;

■ through the tears we see in Ken's father's eyes as he receives the Eucharist each week.

They listened to us before active listening was defined as a skill. They hugged us before there were bumper stickers to remind us. They are not perfect people or parents; they lose their patience, disagree with choices we have made, remind us in subtle (and not so subtle) ways about the traditions of our Church or the importance of raising our children in faith. They challenge us and call us to forgiveness when we are hurt by their words or actions, or they by our behavior. Through it all, we never doubted that we were loved, even during those times we didn't like our parents very much. It was their love for us that helped us understand the magnitude of God's love, and hopefully it is through our love that our children will.

Other family and community members can also be great role models for our children. Among some ethnic groups the role of godparents is taken quite seriously. The godmother or godfather pledge to be available for the child throughout his or her life, modeling faith and providing ongoing support for the child and the family. In other groups community members who live lives of service to the community and show a special concern for children serve as special "extended family members" for the entire local community.

The members of each generation practice their religion in ways that comfort them and give them strength, direction and purpose. We neither judge nor measure their faith; each of us draws what we need from our faith in our own time, place and way. There isn't only one best or effective way of living faith. Just as we may do things differently than our parents, so we must be tolerant of the different ways our children may choose to worship.

For example, we learned very quickly from our oldest child that faith and religious practice are not one and the same to him. As we were strongly encouraging (nagging?) him to be more active in his local church, he told us in no uncertain terms that although he didn't go to church he still believed in God, and that perhaps we were unfairly judging his faith by his religious practices. We have since examined the differences and are careful to be clear in the terminology we use. Has this led to a change in his religious practice? Not yet, but we continue to hope it will. He joins us on Christmas and Easter for Mass because, in his words, "It is our family tradition and a way to stay connected to family, which for me has a lot to do with faith." We are delighted—his presence makes our celebration fuller and more joyous—and hope this connection will lead him to more regular practice. Our allowing for his difference keeps us connected.

When our children were choosing a career or a life-style and were not sure in which direction they wanted to go, we would tell them to pray about it and talk with other people of faith, as well as search out the other information they needed to make their decision. They know how important prayer is to us because whenever we have questions about anything in our life, we pray for direction or guidance and tell them how we think our prayers are answered. They know that their father prays for them by name each day before he arrives at work.

Once when our daughter and her father were at odds with each other, loving one another but not finding the common ground to share it, they went to see our pastor and friend to help them find the way to a better, more intimate relationship with each other. They needed not only someone they trusted but someone who also knew that we are a family of faith. We trust that by living what we believe, our children will begin to establish the groundwork for their own future of faith in community.

THROUGH LIFE TRANSITIONS

When the first of our children told us that he was thinking of getting married, one of the ways we learned about our daughter-in-law was over breakfast after Mass. We had lively, spontaneous conversations, and both of them knew we were concerned about the part that God would play in their marriage. We have had great sympathy for any of our children who were the first to do anything in our family since they are the ones on whom we "practice" parenting. Hopefully we learn from our mistakes which makes it easier for the next child!

During the marriage preparations, we were so excited and wanted our son and his fiancée to be happy and make this marriage work so much, that we became a little too enthusiastic. Looking back, we wonder now why they even speak to us! It's a wonder that we didn't push them away from us and their faith!

After an evening together when we talked about their different personalities and how they interact, they had the biggest fight of their courtship. That's when we learned that, as their parents, we needed to let other couples give them formal marriage preparation. All we can do is love and support them.

As much as we would like to spare our children pain, we can't prevent the struggles and frustrations they need to experience to build their marriage. What we decided we could do is to let them know how happy we were that they would be sharing this vocation with each other. And so, the Spirit led us with an idea of how our family could mark this rite of passage and welcome his wife into our lives and our family.

With the help of our parish priest, we prepared a home Eucharistic liturgy or ritual that would mark the event. Our children had grown up with these ritual experiences so we knew it was something with which they would be comfortable. We chose appropriate readings and wrote a homily recalling how our son had contributed throughout the years to our growth as people and as a family. His brothers and sister did the prayer of the faithful and the readings and, as a final blessing, we gave them a blessing cup to take with them into their new life as husband and wife. We blessed them both on their foreheads and called upon God to walk with them and support them on their journey. We followed the service with a meal that was lively and filled with stories and laughter. We wanted our son to know he was free to leave his family of origin, as he had known it, and begin the new way of life he had chosen with our blessing.

Unfortunately, we did not repeat this celebration when our next child got married. We have rationalized all the reasons why: there was not enough time and it was too close to the holidays. But the truth is that at the time of his marriage, there was hurt and tension in our family. Although we prepared a ceremony, we did not use it. We nursed our confusion and hurt instead of having the courage to step out in faith and risk rejection. Even though deep in our hearts we knew that our children would have responded to our calling us all together, we allowed fear to rule our behavior instead of love. There was a sense of loss in not having followed our faith-filled instincts, and we are trying to choose another time to celebrate their new life together.

They are a faith-filled couple and their wedding was witness to this. They planned their liturgical celebration with as much effort as they did their reception. They invited Christ into their relationship as they exchanged their vows, and we will never forget the silence in the church as people experienced the presence of God at that moment. It has been because of our daughter-in-law that our son has returned to practicing his religion. She helped him recognize the importance of being church-connected as a way of increasing their faith and supporting their commitment as they adjust to being a married couple.

After their wedding there were no more excuses to avoid the stress and tension everyone was feeling. The hurt and discomfort we were experiencing in our family drove us to find a reconciliation. A family meeting was called by one of our children and the issues brought to the table. Each had the opportunity to correct misunderstandings, raise questions, challenge each other's honesty, express their feelings and shed some tears. It was our child's courage that allowed us to do this. If he had not had that confidence, the beginning of our forgiveness for each other would not have happened. Although everything was not answered or solved as a result of our gathering, the value of the family was recognized by each of us, and the value of faith was lived out by our coming together. Although a full healing did not take place until a few months later, we all knew it would happen and we all trusted that God would show us the way and the time.

We are human as Christ was human. Christ shows us the way and lives in us when we have faith in what he has said is truth. "....there are three things that last, faith, hope and love. And the greatest of these is love" (1 Cor 13:13). That gathering of our family around the kitchen table had love as our common denominator. Our love of each other was greater than the pain, hurt, confusion and alienation.

In transmitting faith to our adult children there is a mutuality. We recognize that only in relationship can faith flourish. Parents and children share this journey of faith together, and the flow back and forth benefits all of us. Daily, our daughter-in-law reads a 'spiritual thought for the day' and shares this with our son. On days he knows we are feeling discouraged, he will pull this 'thought' out of his wallet and give it to one of us for our reflection.

Faith has shown us a way of loving. First, loving ourselves as unique persons in God's ongoing creation, then loving each person in our family as unique individuals. We were well aware of each of our children's uniqueness through the relationship of our daughter and the young man she loves. We were surprised one Christmas morning when she came into the kitchen with two slippers on her hands in the shape of big, funny, floppy-eared dogs, a gift from her boyfriend. As she removed the slipper from her left hand, there appeared a diamond! She had a hopeful, yet tentative look on her face because she knew we had some concerns about her relationship. Time stood still.

A number of things made us hesitate. She was our only daughter and the baby of the family. Also, we were flooded with the memories of our own engagement which elicited a hesitancy on our parents' part about our choice of each other as partners. We hugged her and held her before saying a word! (In looking back, it also gave us some time to think!) Her father then asked her to invite her fiancé to our home so we could speak with both of them at the same time. She did as we asked and then disappeared into her room, leaving the three of us with separate worries, fears and prayers. Did we pray!

When we all met, again at the kitchen table (if that table could talk!), we spoke about our dreams and hopes for our daughter. We discussed the reasons why we were hesitant to give them our full blessing, we were honest about the resistance we had in accepting this young man, and they listened with open minds. We asked his forgiveness for how we had treated him in the past and told him we would work on our attitudes about him and support their decision as best we could. We encouraged them to meet with our parish priest as soon as possible to begin their preparation. We reminded them that engagement is a time to think about the decision they were making. At the end of this time they would either decide to marry or to go their separate ways.

This did not fulfill the fantasy of our daughter's marriage. The reality was not what we expected, and we needed to come to terms with letting go of our fantasy by looking through our daughter's eyes and seeing her fiancé as she did. We began to recognize this young man for the person he is today, not who he had been years before. We looked for his and our daughter's similarities instead of seeing only their differences, and we prayed constantly to be relieved of our fears and anxiety. At the end of the engagement, the wedding was postponed; they decided that they were not yet ready to accept all the responsibilities of marriage and wanted to work out a few more issues before setting a date. We are proud of both of them and their maturity in not getting caught up in the marry-go-round of their friends and family.

As parents, we have come a long way. We have come to see our daughter as an adult, one who knows her own needs and is able to make her own choices, instead of relating to her as the baby in the family. We didn't allow ourselves to get stuck in the "parent knows best" syndrome. We also became aware once again of the double standard we have when it comes to our sons and our daughter. Our concerns for her security, material well being and her career were greater because she is a female. Even though we are both providers and homemakers, those attitudes formed from past generations are hard to change. We are now choosing different ways of looking at our children and their choices of mates. Each child is unique and we trust, in faith, that their choices will be the right ones for them.

Transmission of faith occurs in finding the sacred in the ordinary things we do each and every day. However, it seems to be highlighted and magnified at the major transitions of the family life cycle, such as birth, marriage and death.

When we learned about another transition—our children called to tell us we were going to be grandparents—we were ecstatic! They were overjoyed with the news and couldn't wait to tell everyone. We laughed and cried tears of happiness as we went to bed that night. Imagine—grandparents! Wow! We gave thanks and praise to God for the generativity of marriage.

After a few weeks, we received another call, but this time there was no joy, no laughter. Our growing grandchild had died. In our society where there are so many unwanted children, it wasn't fair that our grandchild would not be born. How could we possibly tell our children how badly we felt for them? We listened to their pain, their sadness, and knew we needed to be with them. After arriving home from work, we jumped in the car and went to see them. We felt so helpless and we prayed, as we traveled, for the Lord to give us the words that would comfort them. We don't remember what we said that evening, only our great need to hold them and try to protect them. We desperately wanted to take away their pain, but that was impossible.

We can't take away pain, but we can love our children through it, and be with them physically, emotionally and spiritually. At times it isn't words that convey that love; it's touching, crying and letting them see the depth of our love. Together we mourned the loss of this child, and when we left we knew that we each, in our own way, needed to continue this grieving. That night, our children comforted us as much as we comforted them.

Their grandmother wrote them a letter after being told of the miscarriage, telling them how her faith in God helped her to deal with the loss of her children. She touched their hearts, and three generations came together out of faith, love and shared experience.

THROUGH FORGIVENESS

A vital part of the faith experience in our family is the willingness to seek forgiveness and to have that forgiveness granted. We have been told that seventy-times-seven is not too often to forgive. Sometimes we think that our children will think less of us if we admit we've made mistakes, and so we find it difficult to ask their forgiveness when we know we have hurt them. There is a huge difference between saying you are sorry and asking them to forgive you. When we say we're sorry, no response is required; it is like bumping into someone and saying, "Excuse me." On the other hand, we make ourselves vulnerable when we ask for forgiveness because that person can say, "Yes" or "No." The times we have needed to ask forgiveness of our children have been times when we have experienced the generous love of God through them. They do not take our approach to them lightly, but think seriously about what it means to reach beyond their hurt feelings to make our relationship whole again. We have been humbled and honored when our children have forgiven us and had to be patient and trusting when they needed more time to be able to forgive.

One of the greatest of God's gifts to our family is the ability to forgive. Family life is filled with lots of messiness. Even Jesus scared his parents when he took off from his home and was missing for days! As expected, when one of us is distant from another, it affects the whole family; it's like trying to do a jigsaw puzzle with a piece missing. You recognize the forms and colors of the picture, but it's not complete until the last piece is put in place. That is why the simple but courageous act of seeking and granting forgiveness is so necessary: it puts the piece back and completes the family picture. We release a power within ourselves when we forgive. That act of will shifts our focus from hurt, anger and rejection to healing and reconciliation. A full life is one of wholeness, and reconciliation moves us in that direction.

We could not parent if we were unable to forgive ourselves for the mistakes we have made. Otherwise, guilt, for all of the things we have and haven't done, would hold us captive. We have learned and forgiven our mistakes and moved on with the freedom of knowing we are sinful people who need Christ in our lives.

THROUGH OUR PARENTS

God never promised us that our lives would be fair, just or pain free. He did promise us that we would not be alone in our pain and that we can draw upon a source outside of ourselves for the strength and courage we need to survive life's tragedies and unfairness. "Where two or three are gathered in my name, I am with them" (Mt 18:20).

There are constant turns on the road of life and the journey of faith. Just when we are sure of the direction we are taking, a fork appears and it's time to make more decisions. We can see these challenges as barriers or as opportunities. We can see this particularly clearly as our parents struggle to come to terms with their aging and the limitations of their independence. Faith takes on new dimensions and new meaning with these challenges. Time is growing shorter, and each parent handles it differently. The frustrations come from their fear of not being able to care for themselves and becoming a burden and from watching their friends die and their support networks shrink. The opportunities are found in realizing the precious gift of friendship and family. Jerrie's mom is 86 years of age and still enjoys the friendship of a kindergarten buddy. They have a wonderful time with each other sharing the memories of their life, things their family cannot understand in the same way. What a testimony this is to us and her grandchildren! How many of us have a friendship that spans 81 years?

Our parents' illnesses bring us together as we try to be supportive and loving in the best way we know how. We talk about the conflict of showing our love the only way we can and their wanting to be loved differently. We agonize over bringing our parents into our home or providing the health care they need in their own homes. We seek our children's support by asking for their prayers while knowing we will be in this position in the future.

We know we need to give up some of our independence and freedom in order to make ourselves available to our parents although at times it may be inconvenient for us. We must be tolerant and patient as we listen to the same stories repeated over and over again. At times, we may resent the intrusion their needs make in our life, and so are once again faced with the choice of going with our feelings or making the decision to respond to our parents as best we can.

Our children can be an enormous help during this time and serve as a bridge between our parents and ourselves because they are not the caregivers. They can visit, listen to stories and help them with things that need to be done without the responsibility of having to make any decisions about their care. They can remind us about our parents' sense of humor and help us keep things in perspective. It is essential that we keep moving with our own lives while staying in tune with our parents' needs. Our children empathize with our concerns and affirm us in our caring. How we, as parents and children, pass through this time of elder-care forms a pathway for our own children for the time when they face these tasks with us.

THROUGH SOCIAL RESPONSIBILITY

Being a Christian family means we have a social responsibility as well as family responsibilities. We need to practice what we preach if we want to instill this aspect of Christianity in our children. When we speak of wanting peace, we ask ourselves, "What are we doing to promote peace?" When we say we seek an end to violence, how respectful are we of those who think and act differently than we do? Do we visit the sick, feed the hungry, mourn with the grieving?

Each of our children has found and continues to find his own ways of giving to others. Our son has been a big brother. Our daughter is living with a single mother and her two children, helping her to find a way to improve her life. Another uses the skills he has to help others renovate a house, fix a car or write a computer program. When an employee's son was critically ill, our son arranged for him to have the time needed to be with his family. He went to the hospital to be with him as he sat at his child's bedside and made sure the financial needs of the family were met during this crisis.

Faith places on us the responsibility to care for others beyond our family and local community. This can mean becoming more aware of current legislation and how it impacts the poor or writing a letter to local legislators share our convictions and concerns with them. We wish our children were more involved in legislative issues and have talked about this together several times. We have yet to see much movement in this direction, but since we ourselves didn't become politically active until mid-life, we'll keep on talking with them and hope that our belated example carries some weight.

Many of the values our family holds are based on faith. The way we form our opinions or discuss current social issues reflect our faith and beliefs. We are affected by the issues of drugs, alcohol, violence, homelessness, poverty, equality, racism and sexism. If, based on Scripture, all women and men are created equal, then when we encounter racism, sexism or any discrimination, we speak out against it.

We try not to speak in generalities. If comments are made about "woman's work," we challenge them, even if said in jest. Prejudice handed on from generation to generation can be very subtle and we need to confront these attitudes in ourselves and our children as they surface. As a family, we question how these attitudes are being generated. Are they valid? Has it been our experience or someone else's? In this way, we help each other clarify why we think the way we do. For each of us, choosing the ways we are socially responsible has much to do with what touches our own experience and that of the people with whom we work, play and pray.

Our son and daughter-in-law are involved in a research program which is trying to help women to carry children to birth. There is no doubt that they are in this to help themselves, but they have gone beyond what has been necessary just for them by being part of an extended follow-up group and they hope to be able to help other parents who are experiencing the same difficulties.

We sometimes think that in order to be people of justice and peace we need to be missionaries, to join the Peace Corps, or in some way completely alter the life we live. Some are called to do this, but we believe in the saying, "Bloom where you are planted," and think we have been called to be "missionaries" within our own families and communities. We look for and acknowledge the gifts and talents we have, and enjoy using them every day. We have a responsibility to use the gifts God has given us. When you were given a gift as a child, perhaps a sled, bike or roller skates, did you put it on a shelf to admire? Of course not! They were meant to be used and shared, just as God has given each of us gifts to enjoy and use to help build our family and community.

A FAMILY WELL-LOVED: CLOSING THOUGHTS

A family well-loved says more than any words ever written. In continually living out our values and beliefs, faith becomes real and tangible to our young adult children. Our lifestyle can be an indisputable statement that family life is alive and well!

Parenthood does not end when our children are age 18, 21, 35 or 50. What does end, if we choose, is relating to our children as adolescents. As our family grows, we can find new ways to relate to our children in faith and friendship, with the respect of adults. Our changing family is not unlike looking through a kaleidoscope. Each turn changes the pattern of what we see. And like a kaleidoscope, if we look closely, we can see our family as a new design and array of colors, beautiful in its diversity.

4

STRATEGIES AND ACTIVITIES

SHARING THE CATHOLIC FAITH STORY

Families play a key role in sharing the values and beliefs of the Catholic community. This is done when:

- all family members, especially adults, continue to grow in their own faith through reading, informal discussion or participation in parish or community educational programs and share their learnings with one another;

- families participate in intergenerational catechetical experiences, gathering with other families to learn, grow and live the Catholic faith;

- families make the connection between their life experiences and faith values, drawing on the rich resources of Scripture, Catholic Tradition and the faith traditions found in their ethnic heritage;

- families participate together in the sacramental preparation of individual family members.

The following activities provide examples of how the Catholic faith story can be shared meaningfully by families during the young adult years.

ACTIVITY 1. DIALOGUE ON THE TOPIC OF FAITH

The faith of young adults in their late teens and early twenties is often referred to as *searching* faith. In their attempt to personally own their faith, many young adults experience a period of doubting or even rejecting traditional beliefs and practices. In dialoguing with young adults about the meaning of faith in their lives, the following suggestions might prove helpful.

1. Encourage young adults to be honest about what they are experiencing.

2. Help them clarify the significant issues in their life.

3. Encourage serious thinking about the values and meanings important in the life of the young adult.

4. When appropriate, share significant events in your own faith journey.

5. Observe the behaviors that flow from the beliefs and values of young adults. Use them as a starting point for discussion.

6. Challenge young adults to reflect on and question their own experience in order to continue personal growth through self-discovery.

7. Be flexible. Discussing issues and questions of concern to young adults, even if the issues do not appear to be explicitly religious, can be a prelude to direct encounter with deeper questions of personal faith.

Learn More About It:

Flynn, Eileen and Gloria Thomas. *Living Faith: An Introduction to Theology.* Kansas City, MO: Sheed & Ward, 1989.
Rohr, Richard and Joseph Martos. *Why Be Catholic? Understanding Our Experience and Tradition.* Cincinnati: St. Anthony Messenger Press, 1989.

ACTIVITY 2. DISCUSSING FAITH AND WORK

Work is important. Through work, people provide for their personal material needs, grow in awareness of their talents and gifts and contribute to the well-being of others. In *Economic Justice for All* the bishops remind us that "Work is not only for one's self. It is for one's family, for the nation, and indeed for the benefit of the entire human family" (#97). Christians need not only to bring God into the workplace, but to discover the ways in which God is already present there—in relationships with co-workers, in shared tasks, in the materials worked with, in the goals of the work force or company.

Young adults can be challenged to grow in their faith life by drawing the connections between their faith and their work experience. If they learn to find God at work, their spirituality will be nurtured and strengthened there. The following reflection questions are offered as discussion starters for family dialogue on connecting faith and work.

■ Are you happy with the kind of person your job is helping you become?

- What is your work doing for you?

- What is your work doing to you?

- In what ways do you live your Christian values in your workplace? Is it easy or difficult to live out Christian values in your workplace?

- Do your job demands, workplace values and policies come into conflict with your Christian values? Can you give examples when the values conflicted?

- How easy or hard is it for you to find God in your work situation? Can you give examples of when this task is easiest or hardest?

Learn More About It:

Fischer, Kathleen. *Reclaiming the Connections—A Contemporary Spirituality*. Kansas City, MO: Sheed & Ward, 1990.
Haughey, John. *Converting 9 to 5—A Spirituality of Daily Work*. New York: Crossroad Publishing Co., 1989.

ACTIVITY 3. SODAS—A PROCESS FOR HELPING YOUNG ADULTS MAKE DECISIONS

Based on techniques first formed by Jan Roosa, the following five-step problem-solving method called SODAS is simple, yet adaptable to nearly any decision making situation. The method helps people think more clearly and base their decisions on sound reasoning. SODAS is an acronym that stands for the following steps: (1) Situation; (2) Options; (3) Disadvantages; (4) Advantages; (5) Solution. Although described here as a family process, SODAS can be equally helpful as a framework for arriving at an individual decision. To make family decisions together try the following steps:

Define the SITUATION or the decision that needs to be made.

If the decision is a non-problem (like establishing a new process and schedule for holiday celebrations), present information and clarify the details of the situation so that everyone has a common understanding. If the situation is a problem it will often take longer to clarify the situation. Be patient and ask clarifying questions. Remember, you can't effectively solve a problem until you have a shared understanding of *exactly* what it is.

Determine the OPTIONS available.

The next step is to think of as many solutions to the situation or problem as you can. The goal of brainstorming is quantity, not quality. At this stage, no idea should be rejected because it's crazy or too expensive or one of you thinks it is dumb. Zany ideas can reduce tension and keep creative juices flowing. Set a time limit (five minutes should be enough) and write down everything you can think of.

Select four or five of the best ideas to discuss. This will help as you identify advantages and disadvantages. One way to go about this is for each of you to select the option you like best. (Don't discuss each and every option; this can lead to endless, often fruitless debate.) Then see where your interests coincide. Have you chosen any of the same options?

Discuss the DISADVANTAGES and ADVANTAGES of each option.

Discuss the consequences and practical implications of the options you're considering. It may help to write these down so everyone can more easily weigh the pros and cons of each option.

Find a SOLUTION or decision.

It is important to listen to everyone's reasons for a particular solution. Even if it's not the solution you would have chosen, you may learn a lot about each other and the way each person thinks. Some give and take, or negotiation, will be necessary at this stage. Try to find a solution agreeable to everyone.

Set a time for a follow-up discussion to evaluate progress. This is as important as the first five steps. One of you might not live up to the agreement or the solution might not be as elegant as you thought, and you will have to work out the bugs.

With minor adaptations the process is useful for exploring personal lifestyle, career and moral issues. With such issues, the Options, Advantages and Disadvantage steps would need to be expanded to incorporate the appropriate Catholic Christian values and teachings as integral components in the decision making process.

The SODAS method can lead to good decisions, foster family communication and strengthen family relationships— all very good reasons for giving it a try!

Learn More About It:

The SODAS process is taken from: *I Can't Decide! What Should I Do?*—Boys Town Videos for Parents. This 15-minute video is available from Don Bosco Multimedia.

CELEBRATING RITUALS AND PRAYING TOGETHER

Families provide a sense of rhythm and celebration to their faith life by celebrating unique family rituals and participating in the ritual life of the parish community. This is done when:

- families celebrate the many ways that the sacred is revealed in their shared life through home rituals focused on ordinary family events, important milestones in family life, liturgical seasons and appropriate civic holidays;

- families regularly participate in the Sunday Eucharistic assembly;

- families actively participate in parish rituals that support and complement their home rituals and celebrations;

- all family members actively participate in the preparation and celebration of the sacramental rites of passage of family members through in-home activities and participation in parish programs;

- families reclaim, affirm and celebrate their own ethnic rituals and traditions, and participate in cultural and ethnic celebrations offered by the parish community and the wider Church and civic community.

Families encourage the development of a family prayer life and involve family members in the prayer life of the parish community. This is done when:

- parents and adult family members continue to grow by devoting time and care to their relationship with God through spiritual development programs and resources;

- families develop a pattern of family prayer which nurtures faith and sustains the family during times of change or crisis;

- families join with others in the parish community for prayer and support;

- families draw upon their ethnic prayer traditions in creating their family prayer pattern and draw on the cultural and ethnic prayer traditions of the extended family, parish and wider church community;

- parents encourage participation of family members in age-specific spiritual development programs and prayer experiences/services and connect an individual's experience in these programs to the family's prayer life.

The following activities provide examples of how families can share together in ritual and prayer during the young adult years.

ACTIVITY 1. A PROCESS FOR CREATING SECOND STAGE TRADITIONS WITH YOUNG ADULTS

Traditions and rituals help people recognize that family life is holy. They foster a sense of identity and belonging and help family members stay connected with each other. As young adults leave home for school or work or establish a new home of their own, first-stage traditions begin to break down. In order to maintain family closeness and communications across new distances, second-stage traditions must be developed. These new traditions can incorporate young adults into family life in new ways as they move in and out of family, or involve young adults in creating traditions of their own which help link them to family and faith. The process which follows encourages families with young adults to reassess their family traditions and develop creative ways of keeping people connected through shared tradition and ritual.

1.   Distribute a sheet of paper to each family member. Guide them through the following steps:

   a. Ask each family member to think of two activities or celebrations that you regularly share together as family—these can be special holiday or holy day celebrations, ethnic traditions, ways of celebrating ordinary events or special moments in family life, etc.

   b. Compile a list of everyone's ideas, adding any that the family wants to that were not included on individual lists.

   c. Share together what you can about the rituals using the following questions as a guide:

   ■ How did these rituals originate?

- Have they changed over the years? If so, what brought about the changes?

- How has God's presence been affirmed, discovered or celebrated in these rituals?

- How do the rituals help the family connect with the "world" beyond it?

2. Ask each member to choose a family ritual or tradition that is particularly meaningful to them and share why they consider it valuable.

3. Discuss together:

- What traditions or rituals should you continue to celebrate when you come together as a family?

- How can these traditions be changed or adapted to reflect the new roles, responsibilities and realities you now share as a family?

- What family traditions or rituals do you as a group or as individuals want to incorporate in your separate homes?

- How can they be celebrated to emphasize the connectedness of family members even when you are physically apart?

4. Share personal "next steps" for adapting or adding family rituals into the place you now call home.

[Adapted from a process contributed by Antoinette Purcell, OSB]

Learn More About It:

Roberto, John, ed. *Family Rituals and Celebrations*. New Rochelle, NY: Don Bosco Multimedia, 1992. (This volume is a collection of rituals and celebrations that you can use or adapt.)

ACTIVITY 2. A FAMILY SCRAPBOOK—
SHARED TIMES AND TRADITIONS

As a follow-up to the previous activity or as a separate project, invite family members to create a family scrapbook. The purpose of the scrapbook is a simple one: to help families stay connected with their past and into their future. Among the items you might want to incorporate are the following:

- a list of dates special to each family member (birth and baptismal days, graduations, anniversaries, etc.);

- snapshots that trace individual family member's growth to the present, with an extra page or two for add-ons to keep the scrapbook up to date;

- snapshots, momentos or written reflections on past family vacations, holidays, etc.

- outlines or copies of material used for celebrating the traditions and rituals you share as a family. Resources included can range from prayers and scripture readings to special menus or the location of the best Mexican bakery in town.

This project can be done by the family as a whole, with individual family members adding personal reflections or notes of encouragement to the family member for whom the scrapbook is intended. It could also be compiled as a wedding or home-leaving gift for a son or daughter, brother or sister.

This scrapbook project is a great way to pass on memories and meaningful rituals to the next generation.

[Adapted from a process submitted by Antoinette Purcell, OSB]

ACTIVITY 3. SECOND-STAGE TRADITIONS

Families with young adults share many common experiences that provide fertile ground for the creation of second-stage rituals or traditions. Try one of the following or create a new ritual of your own.

A Reentry Rite

If the young adults in your family live away from home, returning only for the holidays, develop a family reentry ritual. Declare the second night that everybody is home to be Family Council Night, a time for talking together, for catching up, for reentering the family unit. Invite each person in turn, to talk about the best things that happened as a result of being away and the thing that each person missed the most. The parents talk about their year similarly. Then go around the family circle again, asking each person to share something that bothered him or her that the family might share. These subjects can be left on the table for future conversations. In closing, ask each person to share something about his or her need to be with family. The process takes time but leaves people feeling caught up and connected with one another.

A Chair for the Missing

Many families find it difficult to gather everyone at home for the holidays. If it is rare, these past few years, to gather everyone in your family around one table at the same time, gather all you can, then set a place at the table for those who are absent. It is an easy way of saying that no matter where young adults may be in body, in spirit they remain in the hearts and in minds of family members whenever the family gathers.

The Family Letters

With family members scattered around the state or country, it can be difficult for parents and siblings to keep in touch with one another on a regular basis. One family has developed their own version of a "chain letter" to keep communication going on a regular basis. The parents start the process off, sending a newsy letter to their oldest child. She in turn adds a letter and sends it onto the next oldest child. As the letters make their way around the family, each person hears from everyone else in the family. When your original letter returns to you, it is time to pen another and send it on to the next in line. The family letter should not be held any longer than ten days. With time in between for postal delivery, it means a turn at letter writing only once every two or three months. The immediate news may be stale, but it still gives family members a feel for each other and connects them directly without exorbitant phone bills.

Learn More About It:

Lieberman, Susan Abel. *New Traditions: Redefining Celebrations for Today's Family.* New York: The Noonday Press, 1991.

ACTIVITY 4. FAMILY CHRISTMAS TABLE BLESSING

Family rituals in which shared faith plays a distinct role are important as young adults move beyond the family home and continue the process of fashioning faith expressions of their own. The following prayer is one example of how prayer can continue to unite family members.

Family and friends gather around the Christmas table, upon which there is an unlighted candle.

Leader: Glory to God in the highest.
All: And peace to God's people on earth.

Leader: As we light our candle on this feast of light, may the Spirit of God that shone on the star of Bethlehem grow even brighter in our hearts and homes. (*A family member lights the candle.*)

1st Reader: Listen to the words of the holy gospel according to John:
　　　　And the Word became flesh and made his dwelling among us, and we saw his glory, the glory as of God's only son, full of grace and truth.
　　　　This is the word of the Lord.
All: The Word became flesh and made his dwelling among us.

Blessing Prayer: (*The blessing may be read by one person or by a number of people, each reading a paragraph.*)

O God of gentleness, in love you gather us at this table for our Christmas feast. We rejoice in being together to celebrate our joy in your great gift to us, Jesus Christ your Son.

Lord Jesus, hold us close to each other. Unite us in spirit with those who are distant and with those who have died.

In the peace of this season, may the hungry be filled and the homeless sheltered, and may the unremembered be united, especially through your love and peace at work in us.

We remember especially those who have loved us in a special way this past year—who have been bearers of Jesus' love to us. (*Names may be said aloud or in silence.*)

All: Lord, bless our food, our family, our friends. Help us to share our love.

Leader: Glory to God in the highest
All: And peace to God's people on earth.

ACTIVITY 5. AT HOME SEPARATION CELEBRATION WHEN A CHILD MARRIES

The following ritual celebrates a milestone event in the life of families with young adults, the moment when a child leaves home to start a family of his or her own.

Opening Prayer: Loving God, you understand the hearts of all your children. Look with love upon us as we come before you, not without concern, but with great joy, for (name) is about to leave our home.

As a gift to us, he/she came into our family; as a gift to all he/she shall meet, we send him/her in your care to your greater family, to all your children in our world. We thank you, the Giver, for the hours we have shared together, and for the times of still warmer joy—yet unknown, but sure to come.

But this, Gracious One, is the time of action, the day of light for his/her forthcoming marriage. Together then, we pray now for your child, our son/daughter (name).

Readings (*A sibling or parent does the reading.*)

Suggested readings: Eph 3:14–21; Col 3:12–17; Jn 17:20–23; Mt 5:13–16.

Sharing (*Parents and other family members can prepare reflections to share with the family and friends gathered for this celebration.*)

The following ideas could be incorporated: qualities of child being married; ways he/she has impacted the family; sharing of moments of pride or humor; forgiveness for hurts committed; welcome of fiancé(e); assurance of support and love during this time of transition and change.

Intercessions (*Read by individual family members*)

For all parents and children, that they may share in the love of God through their love of each other, we pray...

For all families suffering hurt and rejection, that they may seek forgiveness and once again be connected, we pray...

For the hungry, the homeless, the sick in heart as well as body, that they may find shelter and warmth, we pray...

For [child and fiancé(e)], that they may grow in wisdom and understanding and experience the friendship of each other and Jesus, we pray...

For [fiancé(e)'s family], that the love they share may reflect the love of the Trinity, we pray...

Blessing

Father: Lord our God, be with us now as we pray. Look with favor upon this our son/daughter (name), for whom his/her wedding day will be most special. We, his/her parents, together with all his family, surround him/her with our love and prayer as he/she prepares to marry (name).

Mother: My son/daughter and child of my womb, your wedding day indeed will be mostly special to you, one that you will long remember. We, your family, are grateful that we are able to share it with you and are able to support you with our prayers and love.

Father: Blessed are you, Lord our God, who has graced our son/daughter with life and health so that he/she might reach this day. You have blessed him/her abundantly over the years and have carefully prepared him/her for this important step in his/her life.

All: Lord, our God, bring together and unite all our prayers, our hopes and love into a single blessing for (child) and [fiancé(e)]. May the love they share today be just a shadow of the love they will share in the days to come. Amen.

ACTIVITY 6. PRAY YOUR EXPERIENCE

God's love is revealed in the affection we feel from others and in the affection that flows out from us to others. Whatever the emotion or experience, bring it to God in prayer. The following prayer, penned by the parent of a young adult, couples thanksgiving with a prayer for courage and support.

Kind and gracious God, for the gift of family we have shared together in this gathering, we give you thanks. Mindful of how life continues from generation to generation, we ask your blessing on the changes taking place in our lives and the lives of our children.

Grant us the courage to name and celebrate these moments so that we may rejoice in what is different and new.

Bless our daughters and sons with your gifts of faith, hope and love. Guide them on their journey of discovery into adulthood. Teach us the ways to send them forth with freedom and love.

We give you thanks O God, for all that has been, for what is, and for what is yet to come.

Blessed are you, O Lord our God, for the gift of family.

Amen.

ENRICHING FAMILY RELATIONSHIPS

Families encourage the individual growth of family members and the development of meaningful relationships within and beyond the family. This is done when:

- parents grow in their understanding of the parenting skills needed at each stage of the family life cycle;

- families work to improve the communications, decision-making and problem-solving skills;

- families work at and enjoy spending quality time together;

- families participate in intergenerational family activities which build community among family members and between families in the parish community;

- married couples consciously work at enriching their marriage relationship;

- single, divorced, separated or widowed adults work at enriching their lives and relationships through programs, support groups and resources that address their specific needs;

- families seek support and counseling during times of loss, sudden change, unexpected crises, problems and family or personal transitions.

The following activities provide examples of how the family relationships can be nurtured and enriched during the young adult years.

ACTIVITY 1. LEAVE TAKING

As your children leave their household to undertake the tasks of young adulthood, you may wish to address your personal feelings about their leaving, and share these feelings with them.

Connecting with Your Feelings

Your feelings about this child leaving home may be complex and, at time, contradictory. Sit quietly and let your feelings surface. Recall the memories of your son or daughter's childhood. Allow yourself to feel the anxiety, pain, joy, promise that remembering brings forth. You may wish to write about what surfaces as you do this exercise.

Perhaps you will find yourself chuckling over a time that was a happy one, or feel tears on your cheeks as you recall a poignant moment from the past. Whatever comes forth, allow yourself to experience the fullness of the feelings. When you are through with your memories, say a prayer of thanksgiving to God for this child that is leaving and ask for the confidence to share these feelings with him/her.

Sharing Your Feelings with Your Child

Create an opportunity to be in a relaxed atmosphere with your son or daughter. Start your conversation by telling your child that you have spent some time thinking about her childhood and adolescence. Mention some specific occasions that were meaningful to you. Engage your child by asking her if her recollection is the same or different from yours. Move on to sharing with your child your feelings about the fact that she is moving out. You might talk about the small "leavings" that have already taken place—the first day she went to school, the time she visited and stayed with a relative or friend, or a trip she took with her class. Then speak about the difference between those times and this departure.

When you have finished what you want to share, hug your child. If you wish, you might want to place your hands on her head and give her your blessing. It can be as simple as saying "May God go with you" while making the sign of the cross on her forehead.

ACTIVITY 2. SHARING EXPECTATIONS

As young adults move out on their own, emotionally and/or physically, it is necessary for families to renegotiate what they hope for and expect from one another. Sharing expectations together is a necessary first step toward keeping family relationships strong.

This activity offers a simple process for arriving at realistic expectations.

1. Have family members list on a piece of paper three expectations they have of one another during this time of transition. These expectations may have to do with continued family involvement, responsibilities, religious practices, etc.

2. Reflect on why these expectations are important.

3. Take turns sharing your lists of expectations with each other. Be sure when you are sharing that you are clear on **why** you expect what you do. Ask if your expectations seem reasonable to the other family members.

4. If they think your expectations are unrealistic, listen to why they think this is so. Their input is necessary if you wish to reach agreement on family expectations.

5. Continue the discussion until everyone feels their voice
    has been heard and there is basic agreement on reason-
    able family expectations. Knowing one another's thoughts
    and understanding the feelings that underlie each other's
    expectations create a common ground for building
    realistic expectations.

ACTIVITY 3. BUILDING
SYSTEMS OF SUPPORT

No family is an island unto itself. Having the support of
others who share our beliefs and values helps us to shoulder
the tough times and celebrate the joyful times.

Family Ties

There are both informal and structured ways in which
families can seek support. Keeping strong ties with siblings
and extended family can be particularly valuable. In talking
with each other, we find we aren't the only ones facing family
difficulties and can share suggestions for responding to
similar situations in our own family.

Discussing Family-Oriented Videos

Another way we have recently been finding support is
through the use of videos. There are many video resources
available to address the issues families face today. We invite
friends to the house to view these tapes with us. We have a
delightful evening as we pop some corn, move the furniture so
everyone is comfortable in front of the VCR, and discuss what
we have seen. Other recent movies, such as *Dad* and *On
Golden Pond* relate well to our mid-life transitions. [See
*Media, Faith and Families: A Parents' Guide to Family
Viewing* for additional listings of videos (New Rochelle, NY:
Don Bosco Multimedia, 1992).]

Faith Sharing Groups

Not too long ago we were part of a faith sharing group that met monthly. We would gather at a different home each month and take turns facilitating the discussion. We used Scripture, books and papal encyclicals as our source of topics. We would use the "study, judge, act" model developed by the Christian Family Movement as our guide. We looked forward to these evenings because they generated such lively discussion. Faith sharing groups can be organized on a neighborhood, parish or diocesan basis. They can be parent-only groups or occasionally incorporate the whole family.

Learn More About It:

Fischer, Kathleen R., and Thomas N. Hart. *Promises to Keep: Developing the Skills of Marriage.* Mahwah, NJ: Paulist Press, 1991.

Levy M.D., Michael T. *Parenting Mom & Dad: A Guide for the Grown-Up Children of Aging Parents.* New York: Prentice Hall Press, 1991.

Okimoto, Jean Davies and Phyllis Jackson Stegall. *Boomerang Kids: How to Live with Adult Children Who Return Home.* New York: Pocket Books, 1987.

RESPONDING TO THOSE IN NEED AND RELATING TO THE WIDER COMMUNITY

Families respond to the gospel call to service by reaching out in compassion to those in need. This is done when:

- family members model the gospel values of respect for human dignity, compassion, justice and service to others in their relationships with each other and with others in the community;

- families learn about justice issues and the needs of others;

- family members participate together in parish and community service programs geared to their interests and abilities;
- families discuss how the needs of others, locally and globally, affect their life as a family;
- families joins with others in society to alleviate the suffering of those in need and change the structures that allow injustice and inequality to continue.

Families work to better understand the world they live in and make it a better place for all people. This is done when:

- families model hospitality, opening their home to others, showing how God's love is communicated through family life;
- families grow in appreciation of their own ethnic or cultural heritage;
- families takes part in parish and community events that help them understand the life and history of people of different cultures and nations, and value cultural diversity as a special gift from God;
- families recognize their connectedness with and reliance upon others at all levels of life and grow in their appreciation for interdependence;
- families learn about and join in actions with others who share a common vision and approach for improving life in the community.

The task of parenting young adults for justice and service began many years ago, when the young adults were just infants. Conversations about service and justice issues, lived examples of care and concern for neighbors or others, family decision-making on budgeting and how best to share limited resources with those in dire need—all provide a strong foundation for the task of parenting for justice and service in the young adult years. The following activities provide examples of how the families with young adults can reach out together in response to the needs of the local and wider community.

ACTIVITY 1. MODELING A COMMITMENT OF SERVICE TO OTHERS

More effective than any words parents say will be the lifestyle that they model as adults. As young people grow into young adults and begin to move out, physically or psychologically, new energies can be freed up for service of others beyond the family. Existing service involvement(s) can be deepened or new avenues explored. Time previously given to scouting or sports programs, for example, can be shifted to other community needs. And if pressing family needs formerly demanded that energy be spent close to home, the present may be an opportunity to expand one's service horizons. Commitments of time (and money) to service and social change groups can be weighed again in light of the new situation that parents now find themselves in. There is a better-than-average chance that a strong example of community involvement and sharing of service time with others will rub off on young adult children as they develop their own definition of the responsibilities of adulthood.

Challenges for Couples

As married couples redefine themselves and their relationship during this period in life, issues of service and justice need to considered. What is best for me personally needs to be weighed against what might be best for us as a couple. How much time spent in service beyond the home is growthful for me and for us? What is a proper balancing point between experiences that help me grow on my own and those that help us grow together? As couples work to redefine what it means to be, once again, a household of two, what do their commitments to the wider community say about who they are and what they value? Service, rendered as a couple, can provide a new basis for understanding what it means to be a community-of-two.

Sharing individual experiences and learnings can do the same.

Family Modeling

As young adults become increasingly independent, former ways of serving others as a family necessarily change. At the same time, new opportunities for family justice and service involvement appear. Families, for example, who can arrange to take vacation time together might consider an "alternative vacation," taking part as a family in a weeklong work experience with a group like Habitat for Humanity, or joining with others for an immersion experience that exposes them to the life experience of people in poorer countries of the world and offers strategies for changing the policies and structures that keep people in developing countries poor. The combined experience and skills of young adults and their parents can offer new directions for service and suggest new ways of being family together.

ACTIVITY 2. CAST A VOTE FOR JUSTICE

Gather as a family prior to local and national elections for a family discussion of election time politics. Try the following process:

1. Rather than opening your discussion with a debate on specific issues—which can easily separate people and make dialogue difficult—ask family members to jot down several key values or principles that they think the political system should support or which seem to be at stake in this election.

2. Compare your list of principles with those offered by the U.S. Catholic bishops in their recent pastoral letter, *Political Responsibility: Revitalizing American Democracy*:
    a. Economic and political decisions need to be judged on how well they uphold the dignity of the human person.
    b. Human dignity is best protected when people's basic human rights are guaranteed.

    c. Dignity is realized and rights achieved in relationship with others. Family life must be respected as the primary form of community.

    d. Economic policies should protect the rights of workers and uphold the dignity of work.

    e. The poor and vulnerable have a special place in Catholic teaching. Responding to the needs of the poor is of utmost concern.

    f. Loving our neighbor has global dimensions in the 1990's and demands an outlook of solidarity with all the world's people.

3. Discuss the implications of these six principles for the issues to be decided in the upcoming election.
4. Explore the party platforms and policy statements made by the candidates for office. See how their statements or past voting records compare with the values raised in your discussion.
5. Finally, share how you expect to vote, and why. Listen to one another with an open mind.
6. Bring your political decisions to prayer following your family discussion and throughout the period leading to the election.

Learn More About It:

Carroll, Andrew. *Volunteer USA*. New York: Fawcett Columbine, 1991.

McGinnis, James. *Journey into Compassion: A Spirituality for the Long Haul*. St. Louis: Institute for Peace and Justice, 1989.

United States Catholic Conference. *Political Responsibility: Revitalizing American Democracy*. Washington, DC: USCC, 1992.

Wilson, Marlene. *You Can Make a Difference! Helping Others and Yourself through Volunteering*. Boulder, CO: Volunteer Management Associates, 1990.